D0891786

Individuals and Individuality

SUNY Series in Philosophy
Robert C. Neville, Editor

Individuals
and
Individuality

Brian J. Martine

State University of New York Press
Albany

Published by
State University of New York Press, Albany
© 1984 State University of New York
All rights reserved
Printed in the United States of America

For information, address State University of New York
Press, State University Plaza, Albany, N.Y., 12246

Library of Congress Cataloging in Publication Data

Martine, Brian John, 1950–
    Individuals and individuality.
    (Suny series in philosophy)
    1. Individualism.   2. Individuality.   I. Title.
II. Series.
B824.M36   1984   111'.82   83–5094
ISBN 0–87395–829–2
ISBN 0–87395–828–4 (pbk.)

10 9 8 7 6 5 4 3 2 1

FOR MY PARENTS
Roy and Rosemary Martine

Contents

Acknowledgements

With each year that passes, it becomes more clear that I have rarely encountered anyone, whether on intimate or casual terms, from whom I have not learned something. My family, friends, teachers, colleagues, even passing acquaintances, all have contributed in small or large ways to the ideas which have begun to take form in this little book. However, I should like to acknowledge a special debt of thanks to four philosophers whose insights have been nearly as valuable to me as their friendship: Michael Jones, Carl Hausman, James Sheridan, and Carl Vaught.

Preface

During the last several years, my conversations with colleagues in philosophy have often turned to the question of what it was that first drew us toward philosophical reflection. Partly as a result of the comments friends and acquaintances have made, and I suppose, more importantly, as a result of my own experience, I have come to think that most, if not all, serious philosophical issues arise out of concretely personal concerns. But once such issues have been formalized and articulated in one of the variations of the philosophical language of the western tradition, it is easy to lose sight of those immediately human origins. We can become so involved in the manipulation of logical frameworks, the construction of ever more intricate categorical schemata that the product of our thought takes on the character of some rarified glass bead game which hovers over the surface of direct experience without ever making any real contact.

This piece is to be about the individual, that is, about a part of our experience which we seem more and more inclined to neglect. We have done so largely because individuals *qua* individuals simply do not fit very neatly into the systematic structure of categorical description, and it is primarily, if not entirely, such description which has animated reflective thought for the last three centuries. Since the beginning of the modern age, we have thought of ourselves and our place in the world as governed by some set of laws larger than those that arise out of direct human experience. This notion is hardly a new one, of course. We have always tried to come to terms with what we are not by appealing to some sort of transcendent structure. But in the hands of the moderns, that structure takes on a strikingly different character in that the laws which constitute it are mindless. They stand there serenely divorced not only from this or that consciousness, but from consciousness itself. They lie beyond our reach, entirely dirempt from the immediate facets of our experience, and are as a result at once comforting and terrifying. Comforting in the sense that we think of the world as traveling along well-worn paths from which it is impossible that it might stray; terrifying in that those paths seem to have little or nothing to do with our own.

Recognizing that our own paths seem to diverge so dramatically from those governed by such laws has perhaps been at the root of the feeling of meaninglessness which characterizes so much of our age. That is, life itself has lost the sort of meaning a medieval, say, might have attached to it in part because the world within which our lives are acted out has become so far separated from the most fundamental character of the vital. One sometimes feels like an actor dressed for a certain part who walks out onto a stage only to be confronted by a set that has nothing to do with the part for which he has prepared himself. Our constantly tenuous relation to the world depends for its coherence upon the possibility of seeing the other (here taken as the world itself) as something with which we share at the outset at least some sort of common bond. But when its most fundamental shape comes to be seen as radically different from our own, we find ourselves suddenly lost. The ground is cut from under our feet at the very moment in which we think to make it more solid.

The clarity and precision which we have demanded of reflective thought since Descartes is actually a mode of critical assessment in which we participate at most occasionally, and rationalists of various stripes notwithstanding, something which all of us must surely recognize to be an unattainable goal if seen as *the* goal of human experience. Even the move toward reason does not seem to be itself grounded in reason; our commitment to reason in fact often seems a completely irrational one. But that is no more than to say that it is a commitment formulated, articulated, and sustained by individuals, by beings who can never be completely described or circumscribed by the boundaries of discursive thought. The categories of discursive reason are our creatures, and however much we have chosen lately to define ourselves in terms of those categories, they remain our creatures. We owe them no obeisance, but seem to insist nevertheless upon allowing ourselves to be determined by them in something like the way in which Spinoza would have God himself enslaved by his own laws. We can never become identical with the categories we construct if only because we remain the makers of categories. I certainly do not mean to offer this as a startlingly new insight, for surely it is obvious at the most primitive level of reflection. Why, then, do we heedlessly strive to translate every aspect of experience into the language of categorical description, a task so clearly doomed to failure from the very moment it is taken up?

One answer to that question can be formulated in terms of our most fundamental notions of what is and is not to be taken as intelligible. While we have much to thank the early moderns for, it is also directly as a result of their view of the world that we find ourselves at present lumbered with a commitment to a dangerously narrow view of intelligibility. Descartes awakened in us a hunger for analysis that in the light of the past few centuries appears to have become insatiable. To know is to analyze, and if something appears impervious for one reason or another to analysis, we assume that it cannot be known, or can be known only in some vague (viz. inadequate) fashion. Even in the culmination of German idealism, where the appeal to analysis may be obscured by dialectical language, it finally appears to be, if anything, more fundamental to the project. The speech that "God utters before he creates the world" is a logical speech, structured by the most severe of analytical principles. In the light of this modern overweening emphasis upon analysis, the intelligible is understood to be that and that only which gives itself over to the triadic analysis of mediated principles. All of the categories of modern thought, however disparate they might otherwise appear, are triadically structured. They all represent the attempt to focus upon the ways in which things are similar to one another, and can as a result be seen as standing in necessary internal relation. Some third is invariably conjured up to bridge the gap between apparent differences, and a conceptual schema appears from beneath the magician's handkerchief which is subsequently taken to have been there all along.

And yet even in the midst of the most determined categorical reflection, there remains a part of our experience which seems, paradoxically, as elusive as it is concrete. For while the categories of discursive reason establish a series of law-like structures which bind us together with what we are not, we continue to stand apart from those categories in a manner which denies the possibility of ever giving ourselves over to them completely. That is, we continue to be related to what we are not in terms of a radical separation which necessarily eludes any systematic attempt to confine it within a mediatory framework. This is the relation which I shall call dyadic opposition, and, as I shall try to show, it is one which figures pervasively in our experience as the ground of individuality.

Perhaps our most common confrontation with this relation arises out of the feeling — which all of us have at one time or another—of being starkly alone. I remember vividly the moment at which I first came face to face with that feeling. I was sitting in the sunroom of the house in which I had grown up, reading *The Idiot* (of all things), when suddenly, and for no apparent reason whatever, I seemed to lose touch with everything around me. Nothing made sense. The room was the same one in which I had spent endless hours with the rest of my family, one that I was particularly fond of as it housed my father's library made up even by that time of so many old friends, the warmth of a pleasant summer's afternoon filtered through the windows accompanied by the familiar sounds of the neighborhood in which I had always felt very much at home, and yet I found myself caught in the grip of the most overwhelming anxiety I had ever known.

Pacing back and forth, I was almost overcome by the alarming sensation of being radically and inexplicably dirempt from the very setting in which I had always felt most secure. In short, I was convinced that I had either already lost or was on the verge of losing my mind. All of this lasted, I suppose, for only a few minutes, and as the immediacy of my fear began to subside, to be subdued by a return to the fabric of my ordinary experience, I walked through the house and out into the back yard where my parents were chatting over their usual drink before dinner. The return to regularity and orderliness was nearly as curious as had been the experience a few minutes before. Everything was the same, and yet subtly altered by a sense that I could never participate in that orderliness as completely as I had previously. Well before I had an opportunity to reflect upon the ramifications of this experience, I think that I was palpably and immediately aware that this interruption in the apparent continuity of my relation to the world was an irremediable one.

After sitting silently for a bit, looking no doubt much more grim and shaken that I intended to, I finally poured out as intelligibly as I could something about what had just happened. My parents listened quietly until I had said as much as I was able to say about it, and then, as gently and sympathetically as he could, my father told me that there was not a thing that he could do to allay the new fear I had discovered. In fact, he said, this was only the first of many such experiences that I should anticipate, and learning to deal with them would be perhaps the most personal and difficult of all the problems that I would confront. What I had mistaken for a sign of a loss of sanity was actually nothing more than the first moment of genuine self-consciousness which must carry along with it the most terrifying part of being human — that we are, and must always in a sense remain, radically alone.

I think now that the ideas in this book are in large part the result of my reflection upon that early experience, and my attempt to come to terms with it. If it is true that we are always as much separated from as we are bound together with what we are not, as much individual as we are universal, we will never come to an adequate understanding of ourselves until we learn to take account of *both* dimensions of our experience, and of the roles that they play in the world we construct. It is my hope that what follows will be of some use as a first step toward such an understanding.

Chapter 1
Introduction:
Two Traditional Views of the Nature of the Individual

Οὐκοῦν οισθ' ὅτι ἀρχὴ
παντὸς ἔργου μέγιστον...

Πλάτωνος Πολιτεία

§1

BEGINNING A PHILOSOPHICAL account of any kind is a delicate undertaking. For it is the special responsibility of philosophy to be self-reflexive, to be thoroughly aware of the extent to which its beginning colours and informs its end. This general character of philosophical accounts becomes, if anything, more significant when the matter at hand is a discussion of the individual. To begin in the usual categorical way is dangerous in that it lays open the possibility of ultimately delimiting the individual in terms of a set of universal categories. On the other hand, one cannot entirely avoid categories if his intention is to provide a discursive account and not merely a presentation or display of individuals. In response to this difficulty, I shall try to show in what follows that the categories and universal descriptions commonly used in characterizing individuals are important not so much in themselves, but rather as participants in the rich framework of relations which constitutes our experience of the individual. One of the most fundamental of the assertions I shall make is that the individual arises out of such a relational framework and becomes accessible to metaphysical description in terms of the peculiar series of relations in which it participates.

1

I am inclined to agree with Hegel when he claims that to begin with a discussion of the way in which one's work is related to that of others tends to introduce extraneous interests and to obscure a proper focus upon the immediate task. At the same time, since my project is at least in part a response to what I consider to be the inadequacies of previous accounts of the individual, I cannot entirely neglect those accounts. Let me begin, then, with a sketch of some of the claims which have been made about individuals and the difficulties involved in those claims.

Philosophical accounts of the individual can, I think, be separated into two broad classes. In some, the individual comes to be understood as a bare particular about which nothing can finally be said; in others, the individual is taken to be nothing more than an instance of a universal or some series of universals, a reified universal. Upon taking the first account seriously, one is forced to assume that we can at best merely point to individuals and in some more or less inarticulate fashion insist upon their difference from universals. The second kind of account, while it has appeared in a variety of guises, is ultimately reducible to the claim that individuals are nothing if not clusters of universals, and that individuality dissolves as soon as one constructs a reflective account of what is. On the one hand, the individual, considered as a metaphysical entity, is held to be something to which discursive language can provide no access, while on the other it is asserted that, quite to the contrary, discursive language not only provides access to the individual, but is capable of discovering and subsuming whatever significance it might have.

To claim that the individual is simply a bare particular and therefore inaccessible to discursive thought seems on the face of it to be a fundamentally unphilosophical position. It amounts to refusing to pursue an examination of the individual, and thus is to avoid the basic philosophical task of offering an intelligible account of our experience of the world. And yet the view that individuals are bare particulars finds its base in a partial acknowledgement of what the individual is, or perhaps better, in what it means to be individuated. For the individual is encountered as something thoroughly immediate. To the extent that the individual must always be considered at least in part as a purely resistant other, it is indeed bare: bare in that it is not, as resistant, readily conceptualizable. As an unmediated object, an object whose relations to others are always dyadic in the most radical of senses, it cannot be taken up into the fundamentally mediated relational frameworks which have traditionally been taken to be consonant with discursive thought.

But we do speak about individuals. Even in insisting that they are bare particulars, we assert that they *are*, that is, that in some sense they can be said to exist. Further, merely to describe them as something is to imply that they can be thought about; it is to point to their participation in a ground which is external to them. And given that such a ground is conceptually defined, it must be constituted by the triadically structured relations which make systematic reflection possible. In short, the interpretation offered by the second of the two accounts mentioned, that individuals should be understood as clusters of universals, can be taken most importantly to mean that they participate in mediated relations. In other words, individuals are universal and mediated inasmuch as they mutually participate in triadic relations. Far from being bare, on this account, what appeared to be individual actually dissolves as it is enveloped by the conceptually richer framework of universal structures. From this point of view, the relations between individuals which appeared to be genuinely dyadic and immediate, upon being understood "thoroughly," disperse and expand to become triadically mediated.

While neither of these accounts is satisfactory when considered alone, each exposes a fundamental aspect of the individual. As I shall try to show, it is a mistake to reduce the individual either to a bare particular or to a cluster of universal structures. However, to claim that the individual is a completely immediate "This" does direct our attention to an important facet of what it means to be individual. Individuals are always insistently other; they appear as centers of force which seem to refuse any but external relations to that which they are not. At the same time, since if they were wholly autonomous we could not be in any way conscious of them, they must take part in mediated or what might be called internal relations to the things around them. An adequate understanding of the individual, then, must be one that can stand somewhere between the two extreme accounts I have sketched. An attempt to lay a foundation for this more complete account of the individual will be the central focus of this essay.

As I indicated above, a crucial part of this task will have to do with a discussion of the different kinds of relations in which individuals stand. They participate in *both* mediated and un-mediated relations, and an understanding of what it means to take up both of these positions is essential to an adequate understanding of the individual. The way I shall approach such an understanding revolves around a distinction between individuals and individuality. By "individuality" I mean to refer to that character displayed by all "individuals" in terms of which they are seen to stand essentially opposed to others. Now to speak of this aspect of individuals as a "character" certainly opens the possibility of interpreting it merely as another universal which can be used to describe individuals. But I intend something quite different from this. Individuality is not simply a universal ascribable to individuals, but rather a mode or manner of being peculiar to them. It is a mode of being something discrete and irreducible, and as such provides a ground for the possibility of dyadic relations. I shall claim, in short, that it is because the individual participates in this mode of being that it sometimes appears as a thoroughly resistant and self-contained entity.

Considered in terms of its individuality, the individual stands over against the universal, and as a result, we often experience it as something which apparently refuses to be marked out or circumscribed by means of discursive boundaries. However, it is important to notice that this is only one way of considering the individual, and directs our attention to only one aspect of our general experience of it. For the individual also partakes of universality; as we come to know it, we recognize and rely upon its participation in a web of mediated relations which seem equally essential to its ontological structure. I intend in general to speak to the relation which stands between individuals and universals, and in particular to try to show how the modes of being which I shall call "individuality" and "universality" must be simultaneously ascribed to every individual.

§2

As a means of attacking this problem, I shall concentrate on the work of G.W.F.Hegel and on that of C.S.Peirce. While both Hegel and Peirce recognize the conceptual difficulties involved in attempting to come to terms with the individual, they respond to those difficulties in markedly different ways. For Hegel, in the attempt to construct perhaps the most complete of all systematic accounts, the individual appears to be largely an embarrassment. I mean to show that he responds to this by reducing the individual to a series of universals, and moreover by claiming that the "truth" of the individual is in fact universal. There is, in short, no place in his system for a full-bodied individual, and to the extent that this is the case, his system is fundamentally flawed — flawed not only from my perspective, but also from his own. Given that Hegel claims to have articulated an account of the whole from the standpoint of absolute knowledge, the assertion that he has neglected an important part of what is, namely that aspect of the individual which is irreducible, can stand not only as an external complaint, but as an internal criticism of his system. My criticism can best be supported, I think, by tracing the dialectical movement through the early stages of the *Phenomenology of Spirit*, and it is to that task that I shall turn in the next chapter. However, my objection to Hegel can also be formulated in terms of the more schematic account of his system which appears in the *Science of Logic*. While it is impossible to provide a thorough statement of this objection in an introductory chapter, let me point a bit more specifically to the issues at stake.

The term *aufheben* is characterized by Hegel at the end of the Being section of the *Logic* as a speculative one. When he claims that this term is in itself speculative, he intends to point to the apparent contradiction discovered within its meaning. While it means on the one hand to preserve and maintain something, it also refers on the other, and at the same time, to a certain cessation. In other words, in the process of *Aufhebung*, one moment in the movement of Spirit transcends and supersedes another, at once taking up something of the previous moment into itself and discarding something of what was before. What is discarded, Hegel maintains, is the immediacy of the first moment. Obviously, if one moment or 'shape' is to be understood as being in any sense preserved in the moment by which it is transcended, it must be as something mediated. The very notion of preservation is unintelligible considered apart from mediation of some sort. Or, taken conversely, the notion of a preserved immediate is self-contradictory; it is contradictory not in the dialectical sense of being ultimately generative of a whole, but in the sense of contradiction which, from an Hegelian point of view, must give rise to a bad infinite. It is precisely in the assertion that immediacy must fall away during the process of *Aufhebung* that my objection to the system generated by Hegelian dialectic lies.

For Hegel, in the terms of the *Phenomenology*, immediacy refers to the "thing in general" as it appears to unreflective consciousness in sense-certainty. That is, it refers to an undifferentiated "This," to something not even determinate enough to appear as an object for consciousness. One particular, one "This," is very much the same as any other, and while, in Hegelian terms, the Ego of sense-certainty mistakenly assumes that it is confronted by a plurality of things, it is in fact confronted by something like "Thisness" in general. Hegel supports this claim at least in part by pointing out that while the term "This" is meant to refer to particulars, it is in fact inherently general. And it is only upon recognizing that the truth of the "This" is universal that consciousness can transcend the moment of sense certainty, and in the shape of perception begin the process of differentiation essential to the progress through understanding toward self-consciousness. Or, to characterize the same point in the terms of the *Logic*, immediacy appears only in Being, or in something like pure knowledge, and is necessarily left behind as Being is transcended by Determinate Being in the movement toward the ultimate consummation of Being in general and determinateness in Being for Self.

What Hegel seems to mean by immediacy, then, is precisely a lack of relation. That is, it is only with the determinations which appear phenomenologically in the subject-object differentiation of Perception, or, abstractly, in the characterization of Determinate Being, that the possibility for relation of any kind at all arises. The significance of this is that, for Hegel, determinateness must be understood always to arise out of and to be grounded in universal determinations. To be determinate at all is to be fundamentally universal. This is part of what it means to claim that to know any moment completely is to know the whole, to know every possible moment.

Though it is certainly the case that it can make little sense to speak of determinateness wholly apart from a consideration of this or that determination, from the universals which are ascribed to and evinced by particular determinate objects, it is, I think, a serious mistake to assume that determinateness itself is completely reducible to a clustering of universals. For in making this assumption, one cannot allow a logical space for what might simply be called determination *qua* determination. And without such a logical space, determinateness itself collapses and might as well be called simply 'universality.' That is, one necessarily neglects the discreteness or "self-contained-ness" of particular determinate objects. Though there can certainly exist differences, there can be no radical otherness, no truly dyadic relation within the bounds of a system which can only tolerate mediated relationships. Negation itself must lose its force when immediacy is understood as a lack of relation instead of something which is a function of peculiarly dyadic relations. When, in the process of *Aufhebung*, immediacy is discarded as it is transcended by mediated determinations, the possibility of taking account of individuality, and therefore of providing a place for the individual within Hegel's system, falls away.

§3

C. S. Peirce makes a similar objection to Hegel, claiming that within the Hegelian framework the category which Peirce calls Secondness is *aufgehoben*. By Secondness, Peirce means to refer to that aspect of the world which is encountered as "brute force." It is a phenomenological — using the term in Peirce's sense whereby it can also be understood to mean, I think, "descriptively metaphysical" — recognition of the otherness which is inherent in the relations among phenomena. My interest in Peirce, however, is not confined to the objection he introduces against Hegelian dialectic. Peirce goes on to provide, in his notion of the "phaneron" or phenomenon, a useful model which can be expanded into an adequate account of the individual. The phaneron, for Peirce, is that in which the phenomenological categories inhere, and as such is something which exhibits three distinct facets, each of which grows up out of a particular relational context. I have already mentioned Secondness; the other of these three facets significant to the present discussion is the one Peirce calls Thirdness. If Secondness is like that aspect of things which I have called individuality, Thirdness can be generally identified with universality. The phaneron, then, in exhibiting both Secondness and Thirdness, can be said to be in a sense both individual and universal. Perhaps a brief discussion of the two categories will serve to clarify this point.

It should be noted at the outset that while Secondness and Thirdness are certainly distinguishable, Peirce holds that they never exist separately in fact. It is only by means of the procedure which he calls "precission," a reflectively conceptual distinguishing of one category from another, that they can even be discussed separately. With that in mind, let me offer the following sketch.

Secondness is a category meant to take into account the existence of dyadic relations, where by 'dyadic relations' one means to refer to a thoroughgoing and absolute opposition or polarity in the relation of one thing to another. Considered as Seconds, or in terms of their Secondness, phenomena appear as discrete, entirely self-contained entities; they stand as recalcitrant in the sense that they refuse whatever they are not. Secondness is for Peirce the category of "existence"; that is, it refers to that aspect of things in terms of which they are able to supply the ground for their own independence. This is essentially what Peirce means when he claims that "whatever exists 'ex-sists'."

Thirdness, on the other hand, is a category meant to refer to the way in which phenomena participate in general rules, or in more accurately Peircean language, the way in which they can be seen to "acquire habits." The phenomenon, considered now in terms of its Thirdness, is related to others in that it participates mutually with them in a series of laws and regularities. Thirdness refers to the participation by a phenomenon in the fabric of a community; it is the gradual realization by the phenomenon of its capacity to take on qualities, the actualization of the phenomenon's sheer "qualitative possibility" or "qualitativeness" which Peirce calls its Firstness. To use one of Peirce's most familiar metaphors, it is the series of laws participated in and enforced by the sheriff when he claps his hand down on the shoulder of the wrong-doer. Where the clapping of the hand is in this case an instance of and an insistence upon the othering relation which stands between the sheriff and the wrong-doer, in other words, an instance of Secondness, the laws in terms of which that activity becomes intelligible constitute the Thirdness of the situation. If Secondness points to completely immediate and dyadic relations among phenomena, Thirdness refers to the way in which phenomena also stand in mediated relations to what they are not. It is, in short, in terms of their Thirdness that phenomena are cognitively accessible as participants in triadic relations.

The most important point that I have tried to make in this brief characterization of Secondness and Thirdness is that they are to be considered as aspects or facets of phenomena for Peirce. A common mistake in interpretations of Peirce is the assumption that Seconds *are* individuals, and that as such they either participate in or stand over and against Thirds. But this is to separate Secondness and Thirdness illegitimately. It must be remembered that the categories in Peirce's writing are the categories of a Phenomenology; they are meant, that is to say, to be descriptively ascribed to phenomena, not to be understood as phenomena themselves. They are, in other words, both ways of characterizing what phenomena are in themselves and of describing the ways in which phenomena act or stand in both immediate and mediated relationships. In the chapter on Peirce, I shall provide a more detailed description of these categories together with a discussion of the extent to which Peirce's "phaneron" can be considered an individual.

§4

The discussion of Hegel will prove useful, I think, both in demonstrating the difficulties involved in the attempt to include the individual in a systematic account of experience, and in showing what it means to claim that the individual is at least in part universal. The Peircean framework, on the other hand, can both show how the individual is significantly resistant to the universal, and provide a context within which to develop a further account of the individual. In the attempt to unfold that account, I think that a third context different in character from the first two will be of use. In the work of art, we find a manner of human expression strikingly different from philosophical discourse. And it seems to me that this difference is grounded in the fact that art focuses primarily upon the individual dimension of our experience. In other words, I believe that the various forms which artistic expression has taken offer palpable examples of that combination of individuality and universality which constitutes the individual. As a result, I shall turn in the final chapter to a discussion of the relation between art and philosophy and within that context try to provide at least a foundation for a more complex account of what it means to be individual.

I have already suggested that to claim that something is an individual is most importantly to claim that it stands in a series of distinguishable, but interdependent relationships with whatever it is not. In saying that it stands in a series of relationships, I mean not only to assert that it is cognitively accessible as mediated by such a framework, but likewise to claim for it an active role in the constitution of that framework. That is, the individual is both a passive and an active participant in the structure of what is; several modes of being are distinguishable within it. In distinguishing among these modes of being, and attempting to describe the ways in which they are related to one another, I think that an account can be developed which is adequate to the individual. (It is here that the Peircean categories and phenomenological account in general will become useful. In at least one passage, Peirce himself identifies his categories with modes of being.) But it is essential that these modes do not appear merely to be lifeless cognitive structures, categories reflectively constituted as a means of describing a metaphysical item. It is in part to avoid this misapprehension that I have chosen to conclude with a consideration of artistic expression. If the discussion of the individual's modes of being can be developed within an artistic context, that is, within a context in which individuals actually appear, it may acquire some of the force which is essential to the individual but which is by and large foreign to categorical accounts.

While this final part of the book does not involve doing philosophy of art *per se*, certain fundamentally aesthetic claims will have to be made. The most important of these, of course, is that art has primarily to do with the individual. I shall give a brief defense of this claim, and then discuss it with reference to several familiar works of art. While a completely articulated aesthetic is beyond the scope of this book, it will at least be possible to draw attention to what I understand to be the most important differences between philosophical and artistic expression. And, as I shall try to show, a recognition of those differences is crucial to the matter at hand inasmuch as it will be necessary to draw upon the strengths of *both* kinds of expression if we are ever to develop an adequate reflective mode of access to the individual.

Perhaps the most obvious of the difficulties involved in this project is the attempt to give a discursive account of something which can be characterized as irreducible and recalcitrant. What follows amounts in part to an attempt to find a philosophical language in terms of which it will become possible to speak of the individual without on the one hand doing violence to it by reducing it to the universals of discursive language, or on the other of constructing an account which is really nothing more than bad art. One possible response to this difficulty is to move back and forth between a philosophically reflective account and one which is essentially artistic in the sense of actually embodying individuals. But it seems to me that such an attempt, even if successful, must finally be reducible to claiming simply that individuals exist. Instead, I intend to try to speak directly to the relation between the individual and the universal as it would appear in such an account. I believe that by concentrating upon the notion of relation itself—or, perhaps, upon what might be called "relatedness" — it is possible to overcome the most significant problems involved in the attempt to give an account of the individual. And if those problems can be overcome, the possibility will be laid open for a new description of the individual's relation to the universal, and ultimately for a metaphysical system which can do justice to the individual.

Chapter 2
Hegel's Beginning:
An Examination of Hegel's Treatment of Individuality

Reality is the beginning not the end,
Naked Alpha, not the Hierophant Omega,
Of dense investiture, with luminous vassals.

Wallace Stevens

§1

I N THIS CHAPTER, I intend to develop the claim that Hegel systematically neglects the individual. I shall try to show that there is no place in his system for the individual in any full-bodied sense of the term, and that this is the case largely because Hegel's version of dialectic leaves no room for dyadic relation or radical opposition. In defending the assertion that Hegel cannot tolerate individuals, it will be necessary to begin to elaborate upon the connection which I understand to be sustained between existent individuals and the kind of relation just mentioned. And it is to that combined task that I shall turn presently. However, before I take up an examination of specific passages in the *Phenomenology* and the *Logic*, I should like to make one or two general observations about the aims of this chapter.

First, the objective goal of what follows is not to construct a criticism of Hegel in terms of which his system is seen to collapse in the throes of internal inconsistency. Quite to the contrary, I chose Hegel's system as the context in which to formulate the ensuing argument precisely because I have a thoroughgoing respect for both its coherence and its force. If it is not the best,

13

surely it is one of the best attempts ever made to give a self-reflexively whollistic account of what is. However, the question that I should like to raise is whether it is possible for *any* systematic account which has absolute completion as its goal to provide a space capable of tolerating the ontological structure of the individual. To the extent that such a space is formed and sustained by the existence of relations which can be characterized only by the sheerest opposition, I suspect that one must answer in the negative, albeit a qualified negative. That is, if a complete system encompassing relations of this sort can be developed, the notion of completeness itself as described within the boundaries of the system will have to be modified. Completeness in the absolute sense can never allow for a radical opposition, because that sort of opposition by its very nature introduces gaps which cannot be mediated, which in principle stand over against mediation. The logical space which is described by the existence of a relation of dyadic opposition can in fact be most accurately characterized as *immediate.* It is immediate in the sense that the very structure of the relation is such that no mediatory framework can be posited or discovered in terms of which the items participating in the relation can be understood to be related to one another in any manner other than an external one. The occurrence of the relation is coincidental in the serious sense; in other words, it cannot be taken to be in any way necessary. There is no determinate quality attached to either of the relata — understood now exclusively as terms in *this* relation though they might well participate in others — which, once having been recognized, is capable of reducing negation to difference by dint of its participation in one or several overarching categorical schemata.

What I mean to suggest is that when one considers that relation to which I have variously referred as dyadic, radical, or absolute opposition, it becomes evident that if indeed such relations exist, completeness must itself be open-ended. If, (to use Hegelian language) one of the moments or shapes within the Whole is constituted by its recalcitrance with respect to mediation, then the Whole can never be internally integrated in such a way as to be or become perfectly complete. Completion, at least in the strict sense, demands that it is at least in principle possible for every relation either to be or to be in the process of becoming a mediated relation. The question which arises, then, is whether one can modify the notion of completeness so that it would become possible to characterize a thing intelligibly without insisting that its structure is one of pervasive mediation. I shall try to show that this is indeed possible. Hegel, however, clearly thought that it was not, and this assumption informs the entire structure of his Beginning.

In the Preface to the *Phenomenology of Spirit*, he says:

> The True ... is the process of its own becoming, the circle that presupposes its end as its goal, having its end also as its beginning; and only by being worked out to its end, is it actual.[1]

A beginning which posits itself as purpose must, in its very statement, direct itself toward the consummation of a whole within which the first principle determining the concreteness or actuality of its moments is integration. Whatever is truly real, or whatever can be appropriately described as "actual" only becomes what it is as it gives itself over to an expanding structure of mediation. For Hegel, completeness, the developed end of the process of becoming, reflexively forges the character of its own beginning. Of course, in this respect Hegel follows the Aristotelian tradition. Just as for Aristotle the form of a child is merely the undeveloped form of a man, so for Hegel, the beginning of his system is simply the unarticulated form of its end understood as the τελοδ toward which it is directed.

In other words, the beginning of Hegel's system is only intelligible to the extent that it is directed toward a certain kind of end. And if the end which provides it with its intelligibility is one which turns back upon itself to develop the moments out of which it has arisen, their development calls forth a peculiar relationship between the beginning and the end of his system. The beginning must be ontologically structured in accordance with the demands imposed upon it by its end. Those demands appear, at least in their starkest formulation, in the claim that the beginning must be identical with purpose. Hegel in fact makes this assertion shortly after having made the one already mentioned.

> The result is the same as the beginning, only because the *beginning* is the purpose. . . . The realized purpose, or the existent actuality, is movement and unfolded becoming. . . .[2]

Of course, once having made these assertions, it is possible to go on to insist, as Hegel repeatedly will in one form or another, that the truth is identical with the Whole.

This means that the truth must be identical with a systematic design, and that design is in principle knowable. However, as I shall try to show, his claim is one which can only be made from a point of view which is neither logically nor experientially available at the outset of the road which consciousness travels in the *Phenomenology.* It is rather a claim made from the point of view of Absolute Knowledge when Absolute Spirit recognizes the necessity that it create its beginning in its own image: the very possibility of the completion which Absolute Knowledge represents is grounded in the demand for an essentially mediated beginning. As articulated in the Absolute Idea, the internal complexity of its image is reflexively imposed upon the beginning in such a way that it comes to demand Absolute Knowledge not only as end but as foundation.

One finds Hegel making the same claim in the more schematic language of the *Science of Logic,* where he says in the section entitled "With What Must Science Begin,"

> What is essential for the Science is not so much that a pure immediate is the beginning, but that itself in its totality forms a cycle returning upon itself, wherein the first is also last, and the last first.[3]

The first is as much result as foundation; the last, as much beginning as end. But the question I mean to raise is this: Does the dialectical return to which Hegel points *discover* a principle immanent in the beginning of Science, or is it rather the case that the return modifies and reformulates the beginning in order that it can come to provide the logical presuppositions and ontological ground necessary to support the desired result?

It is obvious that Hegel set out to demonstrate the validity of the first of these alternatives, and moreover, that he believed that he had succeeded in doing so. That is, Hegel is committed to the view that the development of Science itself is an unfolding of the principle which is to be found immanent in its beginning. It is this principle which "remains a something immanent throughout its further determinations," which animates the beginning of Science, and which sustains its development.[4] It is also the principle which binds the beginning to the end, and allows Science to return to a beginning whose truth can only be fully articulated in an account of its result. In fact, shortly after the passage quoted above, Hegel concludes that

> It also follows that the constituents of the Beginning, since at that point they are undeveloped and without content, are not truly understood at the Beginning; only the Science itself fully developed is an understanding of it, complete, significant, and based upon truth.[5]

If the beginning is to be intelligible at all, it must be inherently connected to every other part of the Science, and therefore must participate in the dialectical structure which draws those parts together into an integrated whole. Where in the *Phenomenology*, the identity of beginning and end is necessary to the development of "concrete actuality," so in the *Logic* this identity makes intelligibility itself possible.

It is not difficult to understand Hegel's desire to argue at the outset of his project for this peculiar relationship between beginning and end. Without it, the sort of completeness which surfaces as the formative character of his system would not be possible. Given that relationship as presupposition, however, he is able to go on to claim that an account of the relationship in which any part stands to the whole proffers a completely adequate description of that part. In other words, the truth of any part is to be found in its inherent connection to the Whole. We shall return later to a more complete consideration of the way

in which what Hegel calls the "line of scientific advance" becomes a circle. For the moment, the point I should like to emphasize is that Hegel's description of the relationship between
the beginning and the end of his system as it appears in the
introductory sections of both the *Phenomenology* and the *Logic*
predetermines the role that the individual will come to assume
within the boundaries of his system. The complete return which
is presupposed by his beginning makes it impossible that a
discrete and self-contained entity — apart from the Whole itself
— could arise at the beginning, or at any moment proceeding
from it. Moreover, if we allow him the logical step which bridges
the gap between his beginning — as represented in these sections — and the successive moments he describes, we must at
the same time endorse the notion that the integrity of the individual is an illusion to be dispelled as Science articulates itself.

Finally, before turning to a more detailed examination of Hegel's beginning, allow me to anticipate a possible objection to
what I have said so far. One can imagine an Hegelian claiming
that Hegel was well aware of the relation I have described between the beginning and end of his system, and that it is legit-
imate inasmuch as he means to speak only for the consciousness
which has completed the experience of the *Phenomenology*, and
only as that consciousness looks back upon where it has been.
If that were the case, however, Hegel should have made clear
from the outset that his description of natural consciousness
would be of necessity incomplete, a characterization of this stage
in the development of consciousness which is accurate only in
the light of one of the several paths which consciousness might
take. He does not. Far from such a restricted view, in fact, he
claims quite clearly both at the beginning and at the end of the
Phenomenology that his is a description of consciousness itself.
The Sense-certainty section purports to offer an account of natural consciousness from *its own* standpoint, and Absolute
Knowledge is presented as *the* end, not an end toward which
that first 'shape' of consciousness must develop if it is to fully
realize itself. As I shall show in the next section, Hegel's description of sense-certainty is coloured throughout by the presuppositions essential to his end, and is as a result seriously

incomplete. He discards the very relation which provides the logical underpinning for the first shape itself, as well as for its connection with those shapes which will proceed from it.

§2

Hegel begins his discussion of what might be called the first step of natural consciousness by distinguishing between "apprehension" (*Auffassen*, the cognitive character of this step), and "conceptual comprehension" *(Begreifen)*. To try to describe this moment in the terms provided by what he calls "comprehension" would be to stand apart from the immediacy which will provide the foundation of its "certainty." Hegel claims as a result that it is essential that we "alter nothing in the object as it presents itself. In *ap*prehending it, we must refrain from trying to *com*prehend it."[6] One must understand this moment, he insists, *in its own terms* before he can go on to adequately characterize those moments which will arise out of it in a succession called forth by the attempt to "enter *into* it." The force of the truth to which Hegel would have sense-certainty cling is in large part constituted by the conviction on the part of natural consciousness that it finds itself confronted by a sensuous manifold the spatio-temporal reach of which is as boundless as the complexity of any one of its parts. It takes the task of "penetrating its intent" to be as impossible, or at least as indefinite, as would be any attempt to detail and catalogue its extent in space and time. As such, far from providing the impetus for the spiritual development of *Geist*, natural consciousness represents this task to itself as being at once unnecessary and impossible. Its truth, the power and force of sense experience, is infinitely rich: from the point of view of sensuous certainty, its truth is boundless, and as a result cannot be transcended and subsumed by any categorical schema.

All of this surely follows from the characterization of sense-certainty which one finds in the first two paragraphs. And again, Hegel has asserted in perfectly straightforward terms that one can only deal appropriately with sense-certainty by giving himself over to the context which arises out of its understanding of itself. Presumably, this means that we would err seriously in trying to come to terms with sense-certainty by reflectively superimposing upon it a context unavailable to sense-certainty itself. But we shall see that it is in precisely this way that Hegel's analysis and description of sensuous certainty proceeds.

He begins with an examination of that contact with the world which is for us immediate, proposing to focus the discussion upon an account of the "concrete content" with which this sort of experience presents us. At this level of consciousness, we assert the existence of external objects, and at the same time necessarily assert our own existence. But insofar as we point, in terms of sense-certainty, to an *immediate* consciousness of a thing, it seems that the truth of sense-certainty must be confined to the mere existence or simple being of the thing of which we are certain. We are not pointing to a consciousness of something which "in virtue of a host of distinct qualities, would be in its own self a rich complex of connections, or related in various ways to a variety of other things."⁷ Rather, the thing or fact of sense-certainty is only a *this*, something we might refer to as a bare particular. And likewise, the "I" who claims to have knowledge of such a fact seems to be reduced to a mere "This." That concrete content immediately afforded us through our sensible experience of the world apparently reduces to what Hegel calls the "most abstract and poorest truth."⁸ It can be reduced to the bare assertion that *this is.*

However, the "pure being" whose objective truth is asserted by sense-certainty necessarily breaks apart into two distinguishable particulars or "thises." There is on the one hand the particular I, the individual consciousness, and on the other the particular object, the thing over against which the I defines itself. In speaking of these two particulars as "pure Thises" Hegel means to direct our attention to their apparent immediacy, or to the fact that they seem to deny any internal or dialectical relation to one another when considered in these terms. And yet, he holds that when we — that is, presumably, we "wise men" — reflect upon the status of the "This" in sense-certainty and upon the relation in which the two "Thises" stand to one another, we find that they are not merely immediate after all. In their relation to one another, both the I and the object of sense-certainty must be mediated:

> I have this certainty *through* something else, viz. the thing; and it, similarly, is in sense-certainty *through* something else, viz. through the "I."[9]

Neither the I nor the object can be taken to be something merely immediate if each demands for its certainty the existence of the other. The very possibility of this form of certainty demands the mediation of the two "Thises." Certainty, Hegel suggests, could not be attained if they were wholly particular, pure "Thises." But he is aware that to say this is not to demonstrate that such mediation is to be found within sense-certainty itself.

Hegel is clearly aware, at least at this point, that it is not sense-certainty which has recognized that the particular objects which it takes to be concrete and actual are in fact only *instances* of "pure immediacy," and as a result mediated. The perspective from which it is possible to make this claim may be available to reflective consciousness, but it is not available to sense-certainty. He goes on to insist, however, that there is also a sense in which this mediation is to be found in sense-certainty itself. And in order to demonstrate this, he turns his attention to that aspect of sense-certainty which, from its own point of view, makes up its essential reality. It should be stressed that even from Hegel's point of view, the success of this demonstration is crucial to the coherence of everything which will follow. The dialectical movement which culminates in Absolute Knowledge has to arise *necessarily* out of sense-certainty, and Hegel can only claim that it does if he can show that the truth of sense-certainty's "This" does not in fact lie in "bare pure being." Simply, the mediation of the "This" must be shown to arise out of the position by which it is originally articulated; the "This" must be, *for sense-certainty*, not particular but universal.

Hegel begins by tentatively assuming that the essential reality of sense-certainty lies in the object. Though the "I" may be understood to be something mediated or non-essential to the truth of this certainty, the object appears to exist in simple immediacy. It simply *is*, regardless of whether or not it is known by some I. The "This" *qua* object seems to stand as the ground for sense-certainty; it is the first principle in terms of which sense-certainty defines itself. But now Hegel asks us to consider the two forms which the "This" *qua* object may take: namely, the "Now" and the "Here." The being or truth of the "Now," for example, has thus far been spoken of as the particular or immediate Now which *is*. When asked, "What is the Now?" sense-certainty responds "It is night," or "It is afternoon." And the essential reality of the Now is taken to be obviously immediate. But when we notice that for sense-certainty this means that the Now can be both night and afternoon, the seeming immediacy of the truth of the Now dissolves: the Now is shown to be not only something which is, but also something which is *not*. Since the character of the Now "itself" appears to contain negation, it is as much what it is not as what it is, which is to say, as Hegel concludes, that it is mediated.

> A simple thing of this kind which is through negation, which is neither This nor That, a *not*-This, and is with equal indifference This as well as That-such a thing we call a *universal*. So it is in fact the universal that is the true content of sense-certainty.[10]

The Now itself, the truth of the This, is not to be found in an immediate "pure this," since it is preserved insofar as it is also not-this. The essential reality of the Now is neither night nor day, simply because it is also not-night and not-day. Its truth therefore cannot be an immediate bare particularity; inasmuch as it is mediated, the truth of sense-certainty is universal. Obviously, the same must hold true for the Here. Its truth is to be found neither in this table nor in this chair, but in the mediation which arises out of the fact that it is also not-table and not-chair. Given this account, the Here likely appears to be what Hegel calls a "mediated simplicity," a universal.

Hegel holds that we can further demonstrate the validity of this claim by simply attending to our own utterance of the "This." Though we may think that we *mean* some particular this or that, we find that what we actually *say* can be applied indifferently to either this or that. That is, what we say is universal, regardless of our feeling that what we mean is something particular. The particularity of the object, that which we think we mean to be the truth of sense-certainty, dissolves into universality and cannot ground the essential reality of that certainty as something particular.

If we continue to maintain that the truth of sense-certainty is something particular, and turn to the I as the essential factor of this certainty, we find that the I is also universal. For the I cannot be understood to be something immediate if in saying "I" we can as easily be pointing to one I as to another. That is, though sense-certainty seems now to be grounded in the fact of *my* knowledge of the object, and to be therefore immediate and particular, it is seen upon closer examination that *my* knowledge has no more authenticity or essential reality than that of some other I. While I am asserting that the Here is a table because I can see and touch it, another I may just as authentically be asserting that the Here is a chair because *he* stands in immediate sensible relation to it. Insofar as we are forced to say that the one assertion has no more validity than the other, we must also recognize the mediation of the I of sense-certainty. Or, as Hegel has it:

> What does not disappear in all this is the "I" as *universal*, whose seeing is neither a seeing of the tree nor of this house, but is a simple seeing which though mediated by the negation of this house, etc., is all the same simple and indifferent to whatever happens in it, to the house, the tree, etc.[11]

The truth of sense-certainty is not to be found in either the I or the object. Neither can be held up as the essential element of that certainty, or as the ground for its immediacy, since each is necessarily mediated in its relation to the other. The truth or essential reality of sense-certainty must lie in the whole, in both the I and the object, and in the process by which the I comes to know the object as a universal This. The I begins by asserting the truth of the Now. But even in asserting the existence of the

Now, the I indicates something which *has been;* he negates it. He is then forced to assert that what *has been* is not, and in so doing negates the negation of the Now. That is, he moves back to the original position that the Now is. However, this third moment is not identical with the first since the very process of indicating the Now has denied it its immediacy. It becomes something mediated and universal in being reflected back upon itself. The process shows the Now for what it truly is, namely a plurality of Nows drawn together by the process into one"concrete" universal: that is, temporality itself. Similarly, the Here and the indicating of the Here by the I are to be understood not as immediate facts, but as moments of a process which when considered as a whole determines the Here as a universal, that is, the entire spatial continuum.

In order to make his point in all of this, Hegel must show that it is possible to *experience* the Now as a universal. In other words, in order to be able to claim that he is speaking not only *about* but also *from the standpoint of* sense-certainty, he must hold that sense-certainty in its own terms comes to recognize the dialectical conversion of the apparently immediate Now into a Now which is by nature mediated. Natural consciousness must come to see the Now as intrinsically plural, both in the simple sense that any Now is necessarily divisible (the Now which is day is a series of hours, the hours are made up of minutes, etc.), and in the more complex sense of the dialectical treatment already presented. And in the face of the truth that the Now is plural, sense-certainty itself, *not reflective consciousness*, must recognize that what appeared earlier to be a confrontation with simple immediacy was really an encounter with Time itself. In short, Hegel's claim is that sense-certainty starts with a mistake, and at the third moment in its own development, is partially capable of realizing that it has done so; it recognizes that its Now not only is no longer immediate, but really never was.

Hegel's characterization of this experience is so carefully constructed that in objecting to it, it might seem necessary to stand opposed to intelligibility itself. The familiar Kierkegaardian objection, which finally boils down to the claim that there are some aspects of experience which are in principle unintelligible, certainly takes on this character, and should as a result be discarded by us as quickly as it might have been by Hegel himself. To object in this manner offers no reasonable alternative to Hegel's account, and amounts to a refusal of the fundamental task of philosophy: the attempt to come to as clear an understanding of our experience as we can. Moreover, it seems to me that this sort of objection is based upon a basic misconception of the problem in Hegel's account. That is, from Kierkegaard's point of view, Hegel's mistake arises out of the attempt to formulate a view of intelligibility which is all-encompassing, and his objection of course is that no such view is possible. The objection which I shall develop in what follows is that just the reverse is actually the case: Hegel's view of intelligibility is too narrow. He assumes that direct experience can only be known in terms other than its own, and as a result appeals illegitimately to a reflective assessment articulated from the point of view of Absolute Knowledge. Now the immediacy which has appeared as the single most important feature of this sort of experience cannot survive the kind of analysis to which discursive thought has traditionally exposed it. So soon as a conceptually mediatory framework is presented by reflective activity, what was immediate in the experience retreats into a certain opacity. It seems to refuse the logical structure of reflection, and is therefore represented by discursive thought as illusory. Reflection, or at least that kind of reflection to which Hegel appeals, forms and develops a mode of understanding which subsequently neglects the immediate as something recalcitrantly discontinuous. Put bluntly, Hegel assumes that the task of reflection is to articulate the continuous dimensions of our experience, and is inclined to dismiss as insignificant those aspects of experience which defy continuous exposition. But the otherness of immediate experience is not, as Hegel would have it, subsumed by the continuity which reflection imposes upon it; it is simply ignored.

In saying this, I do not mean to suggest that Hegel is unaware of the force of the otherness of the "This" as it originally presents itself to consciousness. There is a sense in which he takes account of that experience throughout his description of sense-certainty. But it is clear from the outset of his account that he assumes that sensuous certainty is the experience of a primitive, or at best, a naive consciousness, for as consciousness develops toward Understanding, the force, the palpability of the "This" dissolves. Notice, though, that it is not the force of the *immediate* "This," the particular which sense-certainty first encounters, which dissolves, but rather that of the "This" which comes to be understood as a "simple plurality" of those particulars, the universal "This." And Hegel consistently neglects the distinction which must be made here. Just as the "we" who come to recognize the universality of the "This" cannot be identical with the "we" who originally encountered the "pure being" of sensible experience, neither is the "This" which is seen to dissolve in the midst of the dialectic identical with that first "This." For, even within Hegel's own account, both the "we" or "I" and the "This" are constituted by the *relation in which they stand to one another.* As the relationship changes, so do the terms by which it is sustained. With this, I assume, Hegel would be quite prepared to agree. However, if this is the case, surely one cannot legitimately make claims concerning the original relationship between subject and object based exclusively upon the point of view of the later, self-consciously reflective "we."

Yet when Hegel speaks of the universality of the "This" it becomes clear that he is dealing with the "This" itself, and with the use of the term on a level which transcends that of sense-certainty. Given the breadth of some of the claims made, the "we" who claim for the "This" a universal truth must be a "we" already speaking reflectively, perhaps even from the standpoint of absolute knowledge. And the universality of the "This" is constituted by the new relationship between subject and object. The "This," in other words, becomes universal *only* when it is considered in relation to a reflective consciousness. Consider this passage found near the end of "Sense-Certainty":

> Every consciousness itself supersedes such a truth, as e.g. Here is a tree, or, Now is noon, and proclaims the opposite; Here is *not* a tree, but a house; and similarly, it immediately again supersedes the assertion which set aside the first so far as it is also just such as assertion of a sensuous This. And what consciousness will learn

from experience in all sense-certainty is, in truth, only what we have seen: viz. the This as a *universal.* . . .[12]

The "experience" by which we discover this character of the "This" does not arise out of the original relationship between subject and object, but rather refers to a particular way of reflectively taking account of an antecedent experience. The experience to which Hegel refers here is actually a new one, just as the terms of the relation experienced are new. He assumes that the otherness which characterized the original relationship is mediated so soon as the subject takes up a new position vis-à-vis the object. The first object is brought together with the subject which stood in relation to it, and together they present themselves as object to a reflective third. However, what he seems to neglect is that the third term, in taking up its antecedents, must also take up their relation to one another as it stands in its immediacy. For those terms were defined and *constituted in terms of* their relation to one another. To be sure, a new relation between them grows up out of the positing of the third term, and it is one which provides a certain mediation. Yet there is no logical ground for assuming that this new relation is capable of dissolving the immediate resistance — understood as the experiential expression of a logical relation: the dyad — which characterized the first.

Consider Hegel's example of the bit of paper. He tells us that if we examine the things that we say about the paper, it becomes evident that what we took, in the terms of sense-certainty, to be an example of the particular is in reality something completely abstract and universal. Nothing more universal can be said of a thing than that it is simply a thing, an individual of some indeterminate sort. And when we try to distinguish it from other things by attaching various predicates to it, it turns out that even in the attempt to individualize it, we point to its universality. Each of those predicates could as easily be applied to some other piece of paper, and confirms the apparent participation of *this* piece in the network of mediation which is responsible for its intelligibility. Everything that we can *know* of the piece of paper is universal, and as a result, Hegel is prepared to claim that what we thought we *meant* was untrue. If it were true that an individual can only be understood in terms of its place in a completed system, he would be correct. And yet the feeling lingers that we are confronted not only by a piece of paper, but by *this* piece. The question, then, is whether this "feeling" can be dismissed as a function of an unreflective mode of consciousness.

§3

There is certainly a sense in which an understanding of an object — even an object as simple as the bit of paper — entails the ability to detail some series of characteristics in terms of which it is or becomes identifiable. What it means to know an object clearly involves the ability to describe its shape, texture, colour, and so forth. Moreover, one might go on to try to describe the various relations in which the object at hand stands to the things around it, or to its "use" in a more or less Wittgensteinian sense. But when we reflect upon the activity involved in this sort of description, does it not become evident that the activity itself calls forth a new relationship to the object, one which is readily distinguishable from the kind of relation described in the first two or three pages of "Sense-Certainty"? In order to supply even the simplest descriptive account, say an outline of the physical characteristics of the bit of paper, we are forced to appeal to standards and prototypes which are present to us prior to any immediate contact with the object. We draw the object, in other words, into a world of significance, and choose to understand it and our relation to it in the terms imposed by that world. It may be that our relation to this altered object will act in some way to effect changes in the fabric of antecedent meaning, but those changes, if they are to be intelligible, cannot be radically discontinuous with our past experience. The context which grows up out of our past is forced upon the new experience as it becomes intelligible. And though the experience of the object is a new one, its novelty is of a sort which is structured continuously with the old. But does this not imply that the original object was already intelligible at least to some degree?

Of course, as the object is drawn into sharper focus, and its place in an intelligible schema is more clearly delineated, the immediacy of our first relation to the object appears to fade. It fades, however, not because it has dissolved, but because we have turned our attention elsewhere. In order to give the object a place within a larger whole, we must turn aside from its presentation as something purely discrete and self-contained.

However, in turning our attention away from that first aspect of the object, we do not negate its significance. It is only the arrogance of dialectical logic which leads us to assume that the development of a mediated subject-object relation exposes the "truth" of the relation between subject and object. The universal character of the object *qua* participant in this relationship is *not* a feature of the object discovered by the activity of a more sophisticated consciousness, but a character which is a function of the relationship itself. The object becomes universal when it is subsumed by categorical and experiential schemata which are no more possessions of the object than they are of the subject.

To be sure, in the act of describing the object, we find ourselves involved in an experience of the universal. While it is natural to attribute that universality to the object itself, to assume that we have discovered something of its essential character, we find in reflecting upon the experience that our own participation in it stands against such an interpretation. How will we describe this bit of paper? White? Square? Finely woven? Useful? No matter where we begin, whether it is with highly abstract description, or with descriptions grounded more concretely in experience, we must call into play a history of similar relationships, and along with that history a framework fundamentally mediated. The universality which we ascribe to the object draws it into a world of intelligible experience, a world which is structured by similar relationships bound together by the subject's sustained participation in them. The continuity which we will ascribe to the object *qua* universal — or *qua* an instancing cluster of universals — should properly be understood, then, as a character of the structure of relationships upon which it depends for its being as universal, and upon which we depend in order to make the object intelligible. The original gap between subject and object is bridged, but in the act of bridging it, both terms in the relationship are necessarily altered. We have not discovered some essential universality in the object; rather it has become universal in entering into a particular and distinguishable part of our experience.

Even as we recognize that this part of our experience is essential to us, and to the world(s) we construct, the complete separation from the object which was inadequately articulated in the utterance "This" seems to remain. We can put aside the claims of naive realism, begin actually to believe that there are not things "out there" existing independently of our experience, and still the bit of paper refuses to collapse into the rational construct with which reflection presents us. To assume as a result that something called "individuality" inheres in the thing would be as much a mistake as to claim that there is *in it* something called a universal. However, to continue to hold that there is some sense in which the object is importantly individual seems to be demanded by experience.

We must raise the question, then, of whether this claim can be made in such a way that it cannot be reduced to the Kierkegaardian insistence upon unintelligibility and thereafter justifiably neglected. What is it that insistently nags in the midst of the Hegelian account of our experience of the bit of paper? Certainly one aspect of our experience that seems constantly present is the way in which the object, having come to our attention as an other, continues to seem *other*. We are, as Descartes says at one point, naturally inclined to assume that the thing is other simply because it appears to be independent of our will. While it seems to make sense that the paper upon which I am writing is "white" in part because I have consented to call it that — knowing all the while, of course, that it is *not* that in any absolute sense of the term — still that does not mean that I might by some other act of will cause it to be red. My control over my world has limits, however ill-defined.

At the same time, the sort of limits which come most readily to mind are themselves participants in one sort of mediatory framework or another. They are, in other words, limits which can be accounted for within the context of reflective analysis. The frameworks which we use in our interpretation of and reflection upon the world are presented to us in much the same way that pre-reflective consciousness assumes the world 'in itself' is presented to us. While our consent to employ these frameworks is essential to their continued significance, we do not — at least experientially — seem to be responsible for their constitution or creation. As a result, we may be inclined, even from a reflective standpoint (or perhaps especially from one), to assume that the resistance which the world presents to pre-reflective consciousness can be ascribed to a part of our experience which upon closer examination exposes itself as thoroughly mediated.

This is essentially the logical move which Hegel makes in the beginning of the Perception section of the *Phenomenology:*

> Immediate certainty does not take over the truth, for its truth is the universal, whereas certainty wants to apprehend the This. Perception, on the other hand, takes what is present to it as a universal.[13]

In understanding "what is present to it as a universal," the second shape which consciousness assumes — a shape, notice, which is fundamentally, if not completely reflective — retreats from the negativity found in the original relationship between subject and object by reducing negation to difference. What pre-reflective consciousness experiences as a "limit" comes to be understood as a function of the way in which the object is different, *not from the subject,* but rather from other objects. The object can still reasonably be considered independent of us, but it is that as a participant in the essentially mediated web of relationships described above. What appeared to be a palpable resistance thus dissolves, and one is left with Hegel's claim that it was only an illusion to begin with. The radical diremption which characterized the subject's prior relationship to the object is put aside as consciousness asserts that the "principle of the object, the universal, is in its simplicity a mediated universal."[14]

While Hegel will claim that it is only in Perception that the "I" of sense-certainty can come to experience negation, he has actually done away with the possibility of taking account of the sort of negation which is fundamental to what I have been calling the original relationship of subject to object. After having asserted that the object must express its universality "explicitly as its own inherent nature," he goes on to say that "it is only perception that has negation, distinction, multiplicity in its very nature." There is a sense in which this second claim is offered as support for the first. That is, he seems to be saying that unless the object comes to be understood as universal, differentiation of any sort whatever is impossible. The "This," in other words, must become a "thing with many properties" in order that it can be taken up by consciousness even as a sense-datum, but as such it cannot stand as participant in a relationship characterized by radical negation. For negation itself, given this account, appears to be grounded in difference, or the process of distinction, a process which is by nature mediated. Again, given this account, the This stands apart from what it is not only in the sense of being "not-white" or "not-cubical," never in the more fundamental sense of being not-This or not-That, as Hegel might say, *simpliciter.*

Since the point I mean to make here centers on Hegel's understanding of negation, perhaps it will become more evident if we return for a moment to the claim that Hegel has reduced negation to difference. Implicit in this assertion is the assumption that negation can be understood in a variety of ways. From a metaphysical point of view, perhaps the first sense of negation which comes to mind is that of absolute negation. It is to this kind of negation that Parmenides meant to point with the phrase "It is not," and the logical difficulties which appear in reflection upon the notion gave rise to one of the earliest philosophically discursive speeches. Parmenides, of course, concludes that not only is it nonsense to assume that "what is not" could exist, but that it is logically unthinkable. To think is to think of *something;* to think of nothing is simply not to think. A term which purports to denote the opposite of being stands without any definition whatever, and is as a result logically unspeakable. (Or in Aristotelian terms, ουσζα has no contrary.) And, as I shall try to show in the next section, Hegel consistently relies upon an understanding of radical negation which finds its logical antecedents in Greek thought.

§4

One finds a highly sophisticated discussion of the problem of negation in Plato's *Sophist,* and since Hegel himself took this account to be a precursor of his own, it may be useful to examine it briefly.[15] After characterizing the sophist as a maker of images, the Eleatic Stranger attempts to give an account of the relation between images and originals. Since an image is always an *image of* an original, and nevertheless must stand apart as something discrete, it becomes necessary to claim that the image both is and is not the original. It seems, then, that one is forced to recognize 'not-being' as part of the essence of an image; and if one is to hold that images exist, he must at the same time admit that there is at least a sense in which "not-being" exists.

The discussion continues in search of a way of attaching meaning to 'not-being' without involving oneself in logical contradiction. It is established that the term cannot be rendered meaningful by attaching it to any particular being, since to do so would be to deny the existence of that which was to afford it meaning. Nor can the term 'not-being' have attributed to it some other universal (here, the discussion centers on number), since to do so would be to make it determinate. As something determinate, it could not stand in contrast with being as its opposite, and unless it can do that, it must be understood simply as one determinate being among others.

The difficulty which has arisen might be put in this way: if not-being is to have any meaning at all, it must be indeterminate, but in being indeterminate it is inaccessible to logical speech (ορθῶω λογω) and cannot have meaning. Thus the Stranger is compelled to conclude that not-being "is a thing inconceivable, inexpressable, unspeakable, and irrational."[16]

It is the way in which the Stranger has chosen to understand not-being that drives him to this conclusion. All of the difficulties pointed to in this section of the dialogue are difficulties which arise in the attempt to consider not-being as something absolute, something in itself. Not-being is taken up as the opposite of being (τὸ μηδαμῶς ὄν) , and considered as such, since it cannot participate in any form, it must remain completely unintelligible. Upon returning to a consideration of being, the Stranger finds that being and not-being are allied at least inasmuch as being seems to partake of the same difficulty. When one attempts to treat either of them as something perfectly discrete, he finds that they are equally inaccessible to speech. Obviously enough, then, if the Stranger is to be able to make sense of his earlier claims concerning the sophist, he must find some other way of characterizing not-being. He does this by modifying the notion of not-being to that of otherness. In other words, he moves the discussion of being and not-being into a relational context, wherein it becomes possible to draw upon the relationships among the so-called μέγιστα γένη to provide discursive access to both being and not-being. I apologize at the outset for what it leaves to be desired, but the following much abbreviated version of that argument will, I think, be adequate for our purposes.

The Stranger begins by considering the three classes, being, motion, and rest, and discovers that two more classes arise out of the relations existing among the first three. Motion obviously is other than rest, and being must be something other than each of these. For if being were the same as either one, the other either could not exist at all, or would dissolve into its opposite. Each of them, then, is *other* than the remaining two, and is also the *same* as itself. Now, if the original three classes are distinct from one another, then no one of them can be identical with either "same" or "other," while at the same time, of course, each must partake of both. As a result, "same" and "other" appear themselves as classes which can be distinguished from each of the first three. Moreover, and perhaps most importantly, since the other comes to be other as *other than* something else, the Stranger holds that the other must always be conceived as relative. Simply, to speak of an absolute other would be to speak of an other which partook of the "same." This is logically im-possible since there would then exist an other to which the absolute other was not other—namely itself.

In order to be at all, each class must participate in being, but in order to be determinate, each must partake of the "other." The other, then, is seen to permeate all of the classes inasmuch as each must be other than the rest, and since being is included among them, each is also other than being. The Stranger is able to claim as a result that in all of the classes, "the nature of the other so operates as to make each one other than being, and therefore not-being."[17] Thus he has developed a way of constru-ing the notion of not-being in such a way that it can be brought into proper logical discourse. Since every class must partake of being, and must also partake of the other, it is possible to say that in the case of each class, an instance of not-being is.

In having presented this account, I do not mean to argue either for or against Plato's ontological landscape. It is rather the logical structure of Plato's manner of dealing with negation which bears upon my objection to Hegel. In the Stranger's speech, I think that one can find clearly articulated the logical move which remains implicit in the Hegelian lurch out of sense-cer-tainty into perception. What Hegel really means in claiming that negation first becomes logically possible only in Perception is that negation can enter into logical discourse only at the mo-ment at which differentiation in terms of universals becomes available to consciousness. Just as the Stranger found that the first sense of negation, that is, absolute negation, was logically empty, so Hegel will claim that the negativity experienced in sense-certainty is an empty abstraction. From Hegel's point of view, the immediacy of the relationship between the "This" and the subject of sense-certainty makes it impossible that *any* in-telligible relation could exist. It is in this sense that he is pre-pared to claim that what the subject purports to "mean" cannot be reached by language.[18] And he goes on to claim, as does the Stranger, that what is unspeakable is irrational, and (for Hegel) even untrue.

The accounts found in the *Sophist* and the *Phenomenology* are similar in that each begins with a confrontation with negativity. In order to make sense of that experience, it becomes necessary to attempt to characterize negation itself. While the Stranger took this project up as one essentially logical, and Hegel, at least in the *Phenomenology*, as one of experiential description, in each account one finds the same fundamental conclusion. That is, simply, that negation can be understood in one of two ways: first, as something absolute, and second, as differentiation. We are presented with only two possibilities, and given that the first appears upon examination to be devoid of meaning, we are left with the second as the only significant possibility. What appears explicitly in the discussion of the *Sophist* is the notion that negation, in order to be logically understood, must be presented and dealt with in a relational context. Though Hegel does not provide in the *Phenomenology* the logical defense found in the *Sophist*, it is clear that the Perception section presupposes exactly the same logical conclusion. Here, for example, is his description of the "Thing," or what he calls the "truth of perception":

> It is (a) an indifferent, passive universality, the *Also* of the many properties or rather 'matters'; (b) negation, equally simply; or the *One*, which excludes opposite properties; and (c) the many properties themselves, the relation of the first two moments, or negation as it relates to the indifferent element, and therein expands into a host of differences; the point of singular individuality in the medium of subsistence radiating forth into plurality.[19]

The object which was confronted by the subject of sense-certainty has been transformed into something entirely universal. The negativity which characterized that original experience of the object is now accounted for in terms of the ways in which the object is different from other objects, among which, presumably, the subject can be numbered. As a result, the object no longer stands apart from that which is other to it in the way it appeared to from the point of view of natural consciousness. It is no longer something discrete and radically separate; it is merely something different. And, of course, when it is characterized in this way, far from standing over against whatever it is not, it comes to be seen as dependent upon what it is not for its definition and ultimately its existence. Its particularity, its character as a palpable individual, has dissolved as even this character comes to be understood as one which draws the thing into necessary relation with all other things. In presenting negation as something arising out of the sort of relational context described here, Hegel has apparently transformed it into the much weaker concept of differentiation. Given the law-like context within which it has appeared, negation is first and last overwhelmed by mediation; in fact, the claim is at least tacitly made that mediation is necessary to its existence as a logical relation. As a result, negativity is seen to arise out of a logical space which denies it the radically diremptive power of the original relation between subject and object.

It is the way in which Hegel has characterized negation that makes it possible for him to claim that the thing has collapsed into universality. Once he has reduced it to difference, the thing becomes a collection of properties — something distinct from others only to the extent that some of those properties exclude their opposites (and contraries). And it excludes others *only* in terms of its properties:

> But it is not as a One that it excludes others from itself, for to be a One is the universal relating of self to self, and the fact that it is a One rather makes it like all the others; it is through its *determinateness* that the thing excludes others.[20]

The object is distinguishable from others merely in terms of its "determinateness," and seen in this way, it no longer is possible to hold that there is anything fundamentally individual about it. Even its character as a unity of those properties draws it into necessary relation with all other things. It is, to be sure, a "one," and must be in order to be known, but it is now a "one among others," something which appears to have arisen out of and to exist in a context thoroughly mediated. As such, it comes to be understood as something whose relation to others is fundamental to its being. And once it is characterized in this manner, the object is deprived of the palpable resistance which can now be explained away as a function of the universal determination of the object. In other words, the extent to which it appears as a resistant individual is likewise seen to be mediate in character. Since the "one" is "posited in a unity with its opposite, with its 'being-for-another,' and hence only as cancelled," the object is brought before consciousness as something which "has its essential being in another."[21] Thus, as consciousness prepares to move on, first to Understanding, and then to Self-consciousness, it finds itself presented not with an individual, but with what Hegel calls *unconditioned absolute universality.*

The individual disappears from the Hegelian system at this moment and will not re-emerge except to the extent that the dynamic whole brought to completion in Absolute Knowledge can be considered individual. Individuality, when it appears at all in the development toward that completion, is seen largely in terms of what Hegel calls at one point the "negative category or singular individual" (viz. consciousness as exclusive).[22] As such, it is dealt with in terms of the same dialectical transformation we have just seen vis-à-vis the exclusive unity of the "one." That is, this negative category, so-called, offers a kind of otherness which appears only to negate and transcend itself. Though it will appear again in the development of *Geist*, the individual has already been characterized in such a way that it must ultimately dissolve in the midst of the thoroughgoing mediation of the Absolute.

If one accepts the notion that negation can only be understood in the two ways we have been discussing, it seems to me that he will inevitably find himself driven to the Hegelian conclusion. However, to do so is to neglect a third kind of negation, one which stands in a sense between the other two. The logical account found in the *Sophist* points importantly to the fact that negation, if it is to become reflectivel accessible, must be taken up in terms of relations. Absolute negation is without meaning precisely because it stands apart from any relational context. But, once having recognized this, it is not necessary to assume, as do both the Stranger and Hegel, that the only relational contexts available are triadic ones. In making that assumption, they both seem to ignore the kind of negation which arises out of dyadic relations. This is a sort of negation which is not mediate in character, though it, like differentiation, is a function of a certain relation. It stands in radical contrast with mediation in the same manner as does the dyad upon which it depends for its logical existence. It is the resistance, the opposition with which we all meet in various kinds of experience, and it grows out of a way of being related to what we are not which is quite distinct from mere difference. Hegel is right to demonstrate how the triadic structure of difference must ultimately give way to similarity, but dyadic opposition, which by definition tolerates no third, cannot do so. And it is out of the resistance discovered in this relation that the individual and individuality as a mode of being emerge.

§5

What I have been attempting to suggest in the previous sections is that to be individual is not merely to accept or evince a character of some sort. When one claims that something is an individual, he points rather to the way in which the object stands in relation to what it is not. As an individual, it is something radically separate and self-contained. Far from being dependent upon the other for its definition, it seems to be what it is precisely to the extent that it is capable of standing apart from necessary or structural relationships. Its relationship to the other amounts to a kind of denial inasmuch as the gap which separates it from the other is one which in principle cannot be bridged. In the attempt to mediate this relationship, one finds the individual slipping away from his grasp. It is perhaps the way in which the individual must remain systematically elusive that accounts for Hegel's neglect of what I have called dyadic opposition. And while one can understand Hegel's reasons for turning aside from an exploration of this kind of relationship, it is one which occurs so frequently in ordinary experience that it cannot legitimately be neglected.

Consider, for example, the sort of resistance with which one often meets in small children. There comes a point at which it is clear that no explanation of any kind will evoke the child's acceptance of something that he has decided he does not want to do. Surely this is an experience common to everyone who has been around children for any length of time. It is one, in fact, which I suspect is so common that it is seldom taken seriously. It is usually met with force of one kind or another adequate to sway the child to one's will. Now I do not intend to call attention here to the various psychological aspects of such events, but simply to the fact of the child's resistance. What is important about this experience, quite apart from its eventual consequences, is the way in which the child has separated himself not only from the person attempting to direct his actions, but likewise from any effort on the part of that person to supply a context within which his demands can be understood as rational in the traditional sense. His resistance is of a kind which stands opposed to the construction of mediatory frameworks. Reflection has no place here; the child is simply refusing something in the sheerest, the most radical sort of way. While with children, one is inclined to dismiss this sort of activity by covering it over with a series of well-worn platitudes, it is more difficult to do so when one encounters the same thing in reflective and self-conscious adults.

Not long ago, I found myself involved in a pleasant but serious argument with one of my colleagues. My colleague is a natural scientist, thoroughly educated and respected by others in his field. Since it was the sort of conversation which in one form or another is familiar to most academic philosophers, I think that a brief account of it might be useful in making this point. My friend had been reading some rather straightforward idealistic philosophy, and asked me frankly whether it was possible that anyone could take such stuff seriously. After assuring him that many people do, I found it necessary to supply the sort of arguments contrary to empiricism which one generally uses to confound freshmen in introductory courses. It soon became clear that my friend believes in what he likes to call the "actual existence" of atomic particles. (Having had considerable experience in electron microscopy, he pointed out that he knew that these things existed because, by God, he had SEEN them.) No argument that I could manufacture would suffice to sway him from his claims. I offered the standard arguments which from an idealistic point of view uncover flaws in the empiricist's position, pointed out that what is seen through an electron microscope is something which must to some extent be controlled by the structure of the instrument itself, and that people involved in particle physics have been making the same claims for years. In short, I provided every argument made available by my admittedly limited knowledge of the philosophy of science. While someone better qualified in this area might have constructed more convincing arguments, I am virtually certain that he would have done so to no avail. Moreover, it was by no means my aim to force the scientist to abandon his position; I simple wanted him to admit that it was open to question. He would not.

Now the interesting part of the encounter was not the argument itself. I have entered into many such arguments, and with varying results. This one, however, was unlike the others in that we spent some time afterwards talking about our discussion. It turned out that it had not been, at least from my friend's point of view, merely an intellectual exercise. To accept the claims I had made, none of which of course were in any sense rationally inaccessible to him, would have been to alter his most fundamental notions about the world. He was simply and self-consciously not willing to do so. When I suggested that his insistence had begun to take on the tone of a religious commitment, he dismissed the idea as ludicrous. I continue to think that it was not. In his response, he had put logic aside, since he was quite prepared to admit that there was nothing illogical in the arguments I had offered. His position had instead to do with a personal claim about the world in which *he* lives and his understanding of his relation to it. During the discussion, a series of mediatory frameworks had been offered, each of which was summarily discarded. The kind of negation which surfaced, then, cannot be understood as mediate. This is rather a relation which has the character of the child's recalcitrance. In saying that, I hope it is clear that I mean neither to demean nor to patronize my friend's position. It is a position, however, which at least in the context of our argument, can only be understood as *im-*

mediate. It is immediate in the sense that the logical space which stood between his claims and mine was one which, given the character of his position, could tolerate no mediatory third. And I think that it is significant that the fact that we could reflectively discuss this made absolutely no difference. In the cases both of the child and of my colleague, one discovers a kind of negation importantly different from that which can be understood in terms of the accounts offered by Plato and Hegel.

Moreover, one encounters the same sort of opposition, that is, dyadic negation, in reflective experience. Consider the clash of opposing systems of thought. Rationalism and empiricism, for example, stand radically over and against one another, each denying the validity — even in some versions the possibility — of the most fundamental presuppositions of the other. There is no room for mediation here, for the only sort of mediatory framework acceptable from either point of view must be based upon assumptions already denied by the other. To be sure, attempts have been made to find some middle ground between these two views, and a position constructed out of parts of each is quite possible. (One thinks of Peirce's fascination with scholastic realism.) But such a position would necessarily be one devised by a thinker who refused to align himself with either camp. One can almost always construct reflectively a mediatory schema capable of overarching opposing points of view. But since the original positions are defined at least in part in terms of their opposition to one another, such a schema must incorporate rather than resolve their opposition. The opposition remains, and it is again one which must be considered immediate.

It is my fundamental contention that it is this relation out of which the individual arises. Of course, neither the child nor the scientist can be considered to be a bare particular. Each evinces a wide range of general characteristics, and becomes known in terms of such universals. That is to say that each participates in a web of mediated relations with what it is not. However, each also participates in relations with the other which can only be described in terms of dyadic opposition or negation. Since in these relationships no mediatory framework seems to apply, one finds himself confronted with a phenomenon which is at once universal and individual. It is possible, I think, to say the same of the systems of thought just mentioned. Individuality is no more a character of things, if what one means by that is an inherent aspect, than is universality. Each term, properly understood, refers to a way in which a phenomenon can be seen to stand in relation to what it is not. My objection to Hegel, simply put, is that he has ignored the significance of one of the kinds of relations in which a phenomenon can stand vis-à-vis the other. While this relation is one which by nature must remain outside the usual boundaries described by discursive thought, it is nevertheless one which must be recognized and made reflectively accessible in order to give a thorough account of even the most ordinary of experiences.

Think again of Hegel's analysis of the bit of paper "meant" by sense-certainty's pre-reflective consciousness. What he seems to lose sight of is that when one speaks of "this bit of paper," and means to refer to a particular object, he is really referring to his relation to the object, and not to some character discovered within it. (To be sure, this might not be immediately obvious to the person pointing to the paper.) And the reason that reflection cannot dissolve the "thisness," if you will, of the object, is that reflection grows up out of a different kind of relation to it. I can analyze the piece of paper before me on the desk, discover its apparent participation in an indefinite series of mediated relationships, and still, even in the midst of reflection, find myself presented with an object which radically excludes all others. It is not only a piece of paper, but *this* piece, precisely to the extent that I can make of it a participant in a dyad. As such, it is something discrete and self-contained, dependent upon no other for what we ordinarily call its "existence." And it is certainly as much *this* as it is universal. My impression of its immediacy seems to be constant through rather than dissolved by reflection. It is upon a "this" that I begin to reflect, and the thing, after having been analyzed and categorized, can still return to that earlier character. Moreover, I can reflect upon its "thisness." This sort of reflection is distinguishable from analytical reflection perhaps in that it calls to the fore the way in which my relation to the object functions in terms of my experience of it, but it is nonetheless a reflectively available aspect of virtually everything I can attempt to describe. Far from dissolving in the midst of my reflection upon it, this experience of the object seems to underlie every thought that I can have of it.

The claim I mean to make, then, is that while one can turn aside from the relation between the subject and object of sense-certainty, he must not in doing so assume that it can be resolved with the establishment of what is simply a different kind of relation. The logical path which Hegel takes does not supersede that earlier relation; it merely diverges from it. And in moving away from an account of it, he likewise moves away from the possibility of taking account of the individual. It seems to me that Hegel's mistake here is as much logical as it is experiential. I have tried to show in experiential terms how he neglects to attend to the importance of dyadic negation. And, as I suggested earlier, I think that there is a way of interpreting Peirce's thought which offers at least a first step in the move away from this difficulty. But before turning to a discussion of that in the next chapter, I should like to make just a few comments about Hegel's manner of dealing with this problem in a sheerly logical context. While the language and movement of the *Science of Logic* is strikingly different from that of the *Phenomenology*, one of the first important transitions in the later work exposes — and, if anything, does so more clearly — the same presuppositions to which I have been attempting to draw attention. For example, the way in which Hegel speaks of the move from Being to Determinate Being is based upon his understanding of the original relation between Being and Nothing. These first moments are both identical and contradictory in what he calls their "simple immediacy." But immediacy here, rather than being understood as a function of a certain kind of relation is taken to represent the absolute lack of relation. Being and Nothing are for Hegel "empty abstractions." However, as we have seen, what stands outside any relational context must also be completely devoid of meaning. These notions do not in fact, then, represent empty abstractions, but rather must occupy a logical place, at least to the extent that they stand opposed to one another. Whatever meaning they have must grow up out of that relation, and unless these notions are to be put aside altogether, it is to that relation that we must attend. Hegel is right to claim that they are immediate, but he misunderstands this claim to the extent that he thinks to have discovered some particular character in the two. They are not identical; rather, one should say that they *are* only inasmuch as they stand in relation to one another. To claim that they are immediate is not to say something of either the one or the other, but rather to point to the character of the relation which makes possible their existence as logical notions. Yet it is this very immediacy with which Hegel would do away in the positing of Becoming and the movement toward Determinate Being.

Becoming is represented as the resolution of the original dyad, albeit one which must itself be transcended. It is "the disappearance of the one into the other." This third moment of the original position is set up as the prototype of the activity which will animate the entire logical structure of the development toward the Absolute Idea. But if it resolves rather than containing the force of the negation which defines its logical ground, it must itself become an empty abstraction. Hegel seems here, as in the *Phenomenology*, to thrust aside the most fundamental character of his beginning, and as a result, Determinate Being, a moment which if taken as beginning would in fact demand the Absolute Idea as its end, appears to arise out of a logical wasteland. Being and Nothing are resolved into what he calls a "static simplicity," and as such can be taken as a "determination of the whole."[23] Once again, it seems that his neglect of the force —and perhaps even of the possibility—of dyadic negation leads him prematurely into a discussion of difference as the most fundamental of relations. And once having insisted upon this as a beginning, the "line of scientific advance" can indeed become a circle. If every moment is distinguishable from every other only in terms of its various determinations, every moment is both beginning and end. For to thoroughly describe such a moment, one would have to speak to the complete set of relations in terms of which it develops and sustains its being. To do so is obviously to speak the Whole.

But such a whole could contain no individuals, and consequently can be neither logically nor experientially complete.

Chapter 3
A Peircean Model:
Peirce's Phenomenology as
an Account of Individuality

What if I bade you leave
The cavern of the mind?
There's better exercise
In the sunlight and the wind.

William Butler Yeats

§1

EIRCE'S REJECTION of what he called the "new Schelling-
Hegel mansion" remains a constant theme throughout
his philosophical career. He says at one point: "my whole
method will be found to be in profound contrast with that of
Hegel; I reject his philosophy *in toto*" (1:368).[1] However, in reflecting upon Peirce's general position, one soon discovers that
this claim is a bit overstated. There are in fact significant similarities to be found in the positions of Peirce and Hegel, perhaps
the most obvious of which is the tripartite character of their
thought. Shortly after having made the assertion quoted above,
Peirce himself refers to a "certain sympathy" for the Hegelian
system in the light of what he calls its "threefold divisions." He
does not really reject Hegel's system out of hand, but rather
objects to what he considers an important deficiency which
appears as it is brought to completion. While this objection is
never stated in any very thorough way, I think it reasonable to
claim that he objects to Hegel on much the same grounds that
I attempted to detail in the last chapter. Let me begin, then,
with a brief account of Peirce's criticism.

In the midst of a discussion of his own phenomenology, Peirce
claims that if Hegel had noticed

a very few circumstances, he would himself have been led to revolutionize his system. One of these is the double division or dichotomy of the second idea of the triad. He has usually overlooked external Secondness altogether. In other words, he has committed the trifling oversight of forgetting that there is a real world with real actions and reactions. (1.368)

Despite his rather flippant tone, Peirce points here to what he took to be the central flaw in the Hegelian account of experience. While he was attracted by the logical coherence of absolute idealism (especially in the hands of Hegel, to whom, surprisingly enough, he once referred as "possibly the greatest of philosophers"), it still seemed to him that however elegant the framework, it could not account for our experience of radical opposition. And it should go without saying that this is not the objection of a naive realist; laws figure in Peirce's system as things which are to be considered quite real: indeed, on some interpretations, as being more real than anything else. In speaking of "external Secondness" here, he means to point to those moments in perfectly ordinary experience when we are confronted by what he often calls "brute fact." "The second idea of the triad" enters our experience of the world every time we are brought up short by the absolute opposition contained in its "dichotomy." And it is this aspect of our experience which he thinks Hegel ignores.

This objection differs in a variety of ways from my claim that there is no place in Hegel's system for the individual. However, as I have already suggested, it is based upon essentially the same point. Peirce holds that Hegel was so immersed in "thirdness," by which he means to refer to the category of triadically mediated relations, that he came to "regard Category the Third as the only true one. For in the Hegelian system the other two are only introduced in order to be *aufgehoben*." (5.79) The "other two" categories are, of course, Firstness and Secondness. Firstness, the category of "qualitative possibility," remains rather vaguely defined in Peirce's thought. That this is the case is certainly due, in part, to the nature of the category itself. But I think that

its indefinite contours actually arose out of Peirce's uncertainty
with respect to the structure of Firstness. It may well be that
he needed it more as a logical place-holder than as a category
essential to the development of his system. But since this is a
matter of interpretative speculation, and since the relative status
of Firstness has no immediate application to the position I intend to develop in this chapter, I shall say no more of it here.

Secondness, on the other hand, the category of "actual existence," of "brute force," or of "real actions and reactions," is absolutely central both to Peirce's position as a whole and to its
efficacy as a model for a discursive account of the individual.
In terms of his general position, Peirce repeatedly insists that
attention to Secondness is essential to any adequate description
of what is. This turns out to mean not only that Secondness is
an essential characteristic of any phenomenon, but also that
without it, Thirdness degenerates into an empty abstraction.
Thus when he objects to Hegel on the ground that Secondness
is *aufgehoben* in his system, his objection is a stronger one than
it might at first appear to be. That is, he does not mean simply
that Hegel has left something out, the subsequent addition of
which could complete his system. For from Peirce's point of
view, Hegel has, in neglecting Secondness, also made it impossible that his system could offer an adequate account of the
"Third Category." The following is perhaps the most straightforward statement of this position:

> But what is required for the idea of a genuine Thirdness is an
> independent solid Secondness and not a Secondness that is a
> mere corollary of an unfounded and inconceivable Thirdness.
> (5.91)

If it is abstracted from the category of actual existence, as
Hegel suggests it must be, the category of universality stands
without any foundation; the universals by which it is constituted
are reduced to barren concepts which have no necessary relation to the world they supposedly interpret and describe. To
make the same point in logical terms, one might say that the
triad can be only artificially separated from the dyad upon which

it depends for its logical evolution. Without the second moment, the third is reduced to a first which, since it could have any meaning whatever, logically has none. (It is this sort of mistake, in fact, which Peirce thought led Hegel to identify Being with Nothing at the beginning of his *Logic*.) As a result, Secondness appears as an irreducible element of Peirce's metaphysical position. It should be noted immediately, however, that this is not to say that it occupies a role *superior* to that of Thirdness. Rather, it means simply that for Peirce, the relation between these two categories is essential to each of them; without Thirdness, Secondness would be inaccessible, that is, unintelligible and without meaning. But Thirdness would also be devoid of meaning if abstracted from Secondness, for it would lack the condition of determination in actual consequences.

I think that Peirce's objection here is clear enough. What continues to be unclear is how Peirce understood this objection to function in terms of the relation between his own position and traditional idealism. His claim that a "genuine Thirdness" can only appear in a system which presents at the same time "an independent solid Secondness" can be (and has been, as a matter of fact) interpreted as a first move in the direction of nominalistic realism.[2] While I think that it is a serious mistake to interpret Peirce in this way, it is an understandable one. Peirce never makes the relationship between Secondness and Thirdness as clear as he might, and if one focuses upon certain passages to the exclusion of others, his position does appear to be merely another version of realism. For example, the passage now being considered, if taken alone, could be interpreted to mean that Secondness assumes a role which is somehow prior or primary relative to Thirdness in Peirce's general scheme. And this passage, as we shall see, is by no means the only one which makes such an interpretation possible.

Now if this interpretation is not altogether unreasonable, it becomes unacceptable in light of the fact that one can find an equal number of passages which, again, if considered alone, make it possible to claim that Peirce was an idealist. He was in fact very much attracted to the role which law is seen to play within an idealistic context. In cosmological terms, he understood law or a system of law as that toward which what is must be evolving if the universe is an intelligible one. The so-called "Final Opinion," which Peirce sometimes identifies with reality, can be understood on at least one interpretation as nothing more than such a series of laws. Given this interpretation, it is tempting to conclude that Peirce's position is finally reducible to a sort of unsystematic reiteration of Hegel's. After all, Peirce himself claims that his philosophy "resuscitates Hegelism, though in a strange costume." (1.40) One need only consider this in connection with his earlier rejection of Hegel's philosophy "*in toto*" in order to understand the view that Peirce's philosophy is shot through with ambiguity.

There is indeed a certain ambiguity to be found in Peirce's thought, but I am convinced that it does not arise out of a fundamental inconsistency. It is simply the case that Peirce found elements in both realism and idealism which seemed to him to be necessary in a satisfactory description of our experience of the world. He was at the same time well aware of the difficulties involved in trying to maintain either of these positions to the exclusion of the other. As a result, he ends in being neither realist nor idealist, but in a sense both, and in occupying this unusual standpoint, he presents a third position which cannot be legitimately reduced to either of the earlier ones. That is, he offers a position which can draw together both the universal and the individual dimensions of our experience.

Since much of the confusion concerning Peirce's philosophy seems to arise out of a misunderstanding of the relation between Secondness and Thirdness, a large part of this chapter will be devoted to a closer examination of this relation. I shall begin my discussion by considering the views offered by John F. Boler and Gresham Riley, two recent interpreters of Peirce's understanding of this issue. While they come to entirely different conclusions about the main intent of Peirce's thought, the views which they present are representative of what I take to be a common misinterpretation of Peirce. Both Boler and Riley attempt to place Peirce within the parameters of traditional philosophical positions, the one claiming finally that he is an idealist and that universality is his fundamental category, the other that he is a realist and that individuality is more fundamental. In doing so, it seems to me that both ignore the fact that Peirce is using the term 'category' in a way which differs significantly from its conventional use. For Peirce, Secondness and Thirdness are meant to describe two different ways in which phenomena can be related to one another. They are neither phenomena themselves nor classes of phenomena, and the relation between them must *not* be understood (except, perhaps, *via* prescission) as an hierarchical one. (1.353) Peirce's "categories" are pervasive and necessary aspects of phenomena, and he has no interest in claiming that one is in any sense more important than the other. I shall try to show that if we focus upon the *relational* character of Peirce's categories, his position can be seen as a way of consolidating (though *not* resolving) the apparent conflicts of the two most important strands of western thought. And it is as such that I think it can be used as the first step toward the development of a satisfactory account of the individual.

One point remains to be made before turning to the discussion of Boler and Riley. While it should already be clear that I do not think of Secondness as something like the class of all individuals, it is nevertheless this "category" which Peirce seems to connect with the notion of individuality. Since the relation of Secondness to the individual will figure importantly in much of what follows, it will be well at the outset to say something of the character of that relation. Though Peirce never explicitly links the individual with Secondness, it becomes clear after examining what he does say about each that such a relation is intended. For example, he says at one point that, "Whatever exists *ex-sists*, that is, really acts upon other existents, so obtains a self-identity, and is definitely individual." (5.429) And again, in another context:

> The point to be remarked is that the qualities of the individual thing however permanent they may be neither help nor hinder its identical existence. However permanent and peculiar those qualities may be, they are but *accidents;* they are not involved in the mode of being of the thing; for the mode of being of the individual thing is existence; and existence lies in opposition merely. (1.458)

Now it is clear in these two passages that Peirce's notion of the individual or of individuality is intimately bound up with opposition and existence. And these latter notions are commonly used in his characterization of the category of Secondness. Peirce insists upon the presence of palpable otherness in the world, upon the force which arises out of and is exhibited by dyadic relations. The notion of struggle or of radical otherness is what he means to point to in emphasizing that "whatever exists, *ex-sists*."[3] And it is in this struggle or opposition that existent individuals come to be defined. For Peirce, it is gratuitous to claim that individuals exist. To be individual is *necessarily* to exist, and to exist is to be individual. Moreover, it should be noticed that the existence of individuals is not dependent upon our knowledge of them; they cannot be reduced to the universals by which they are characterized as we come to know them. At the same time, they cannot be wholly separated from universals, for as such they would be divorced from the intelligible. Thus, at least one facet of the development of the relation between Secondness and Thirdness is the attempt to draw the individual into a reflectively accessible framework. Hegel was right in emphasizing this point. However, as I shall try to make clear in what follows, Peirce realized that Hegel did so at the expense of the individual. In Peirce's system, by contrast, universality and individuality appear as distinguishable but equally essential elements in an account of concrete experience.

§2

In his book, *Charles Peirce and Scholastic Realism,* John Boler offers an interpretation of Peirce's understanding of the relation between the universal and the individual which is based largely upon Peirce's rejection of the position first articulated by Duns Scotus.[4] Boler represents Scotus as holding that the individual can only be intelligible insofar as it can in some sense contain the universal. However, inasmuch as he was aware of the difficulties Plato encountered in his attempt to give an account of how the individual can partake of the universal, Scotus decided that it was necessary to distinguish between two kinds of universals.

He held that it is possible to think of the universal as being either an "*unum in multis*" on the one hand, or an "*unum de multis*" on the other. That is, a universal can be understood either as a one which is actually *in* many, or as a one which is simply *predicable* of many. If the intelligibility of the individual were dependent upon the second kind of relation to universals, it would be impossible to account for individuality itself. Or, simply put, the individuality of Socrates cannot be accounted for in terms of universals which might be predicated of any number of other individuals. For then the individual would be reducible to a certain clustering of universals, and would itself dissolve into a set of universals. Scotus thought that if one chose instead to understand the universal as an "*unum in multis*," or as what he called a "Common Nature," this difficulty could be overcome.

The Common Nature, while it is in many, is not predicable of many. It is in fact neither universal — at least in the Platonic sense— nor individual, for it lacks numerical unity.[5] As Boler has it:

> The Common Nature lacks a numerical unity precisely because it can be real without being determined to exist in any one thing. Although individuated in any existent thing — in Socrates, the nature is his in the sense of being this nature rather than that — the nature is of itself indeterminant [sic] with respect to this or that.[6]

Because it is in this sense indeterminate, the Common Nature can be understood to be individuated in existent things without raising the problem of whether or not it must surrender some determinate unity which it has of itself. For Scotus, all that was necessary was to supply some process whereby the nature was individuated. He called this process or operation "contraction," and the principle of individuation "haecceity." Every individual thing, then, has a Common Nature, and an "haecceity," or the principle by which that nature has been contracted to the mode of individuality.

Scotus held that the Common Nature is possessed of what he called a "metaphysical mode of reality." It is real in the sense of serving as the ground for both the individuated nature of an existent thing, and the "universals in act" or predicables which exist in our minds and are ascribed to individuals. However, the Common Nature is only available to us as something individuated. That is, we only become aware of a Common Nature after — here, in the logical and not the temporal sense — it has been contracted by the haecceity of a given individual. It is apparently always coupled with an haecceity, and is in fact only *formally* distinct from that haecceity. (In saying that one thing is "formally distinct" from another, Scotus means that it is conceivable without the other, though inseparable from it "even by divine power." This seems to be a distinction very like that which Peirce would call "prescission.")

It is clear from all of this that Scotus strongly emphasized the individual, and might be taken to have denigrated the status of the universal. For Peirce, at any rate, Scotus' position suggested something much too close to nominalism.

> Even Duns Scotus is too nominalistic when he says that universals are contracted to the mode of individuality in singulars, meaning as he does, by singulars, ordinary existing things. The pragmaticist cannot admit that. (8.208)

Boler places a great deal of weight upon this statement in the ensuing anlysis of Peirce's position. He takes it to mean that Peirce not only denies the principle of contraction, but in so doing, denies altogether the intelligibility and importance of the individual. Boler claims that "the denigration of the individual is no mere by-product of Peirce's theory: it is just what he wants," and that "ultimately individuals [here, persons] are for Peirce living laws and thus essentially general."[7] He goes on to hold that Pierce insists that the universal and the individual should be considered to be separate and discrete aspects of reality.

Peirce can — and does, by denying within the Scotistic framework
the idea of contraction in the individual — deny that the general
is ever, in any sense a part of the individual.[8]

Boler's argument can be briefly summarized as follows: Since
Peirce refuses the contraction of the Common Nature in the
individual as proposed by Scotus, he must hold against Scotus
that the universal is not only entirely separate from, but superior
— in both an ontological and epistemological sense — to the
individual. This argument can be transcribed into the terms of
Peirce's three categories in this way: Boler understands Secondness, the category of brute, actual fact or existence to be
equivalent to the individual; Thirdness, the category of law or
the cognitive, is from his point of view more or less the same
as the Scotistic Common Nature, the universal. Thirdness, then,
given Boler's analysis, is seen as much more important than
Secondness for Peirce. Boler concludes that within the Peircean
framework, the individual is overwhelmed by the general, and
he complains that he can "find no place" in the Peircean categories for "things."[9] And, of course, if Boler is right, Peirce seems
to have fallen prey to just the sort of idealistic stance which, as
we have seen, he was at pains to deny.

As I have already suggested, I think that Boler's response is
based upon a fundamental misinterpretation of Peirce. But before I say any more of that, I should like to turn to the objection
which Gresham Riley lodges against Boler. In his paper, "Peirce's
Theory of Individuals," Riley attempts to defend the significance
which Peirce attached to the individual against not only Boler's
position, but likewise against the interpretations of Paul Weiss
and Richard Bernstein.[10] Riley represents all three as holding
that the individual simply does not figure importantly in Peirce's
philosophy. But while Bernstein only says that the individual
"always seemed to be a source of intellectual embarassment for
Peirce," both Weiss and Boler interpret Peirce as denying its
existence. Riley, of course, is most interested in refuting this
stronger claim, and turns his attention primarily to Boler whose
argument he seems to take as the most extreme of the three.
He claims that Boler attempts to deny the existence of the in-

dividual in Peirce's thought in the broadest possible sense. That is, Boler uses the term 'individual' in the generic sense, as does Riley, and does not focus his attention specifically upon the human individual — which both Bernstein and Weiss take as their primary concern. To deny the conclusions reached by Boler, then, is obviously to deny the conclusion of Bernstein and Weiss as well, and it is to this project that most of Riley's paper is devoted. Let me offer a brief recapitulation of his argument.

Riley holds that:

> To deny that individuals exist would be for Peirce a repudiation of Secondness. Even to minimize the importance of individuals would be a move that would reverberate throughout Peirce's philosophy, especially his metaphysics.[11]

His basic argument against Boler is that law, or Thirdness, and its instances, or Secondness, are so intimately linked for Peirce that it is impossible to deny the significance of one without undermining the other. In fact, Thirdness, he claims, presupposes Secondness, and simply could not be experienced without the independent existence of Secondness. As important evidence in defense of this claim, Riley refers to the same passage concerning an "independent solid Secondness" quoted and discussed above. He will go on to develop his interpretation of this passage in a way which I am inclined to dismiss as inconsistent with Peirce's fully developed position. Nevertheless, I think that it does stand as clear evidence against the interpretation which Boler suggests.

Moreover, Riley claims that if Peirce were to allow the individual to fall to a position of insignificance, he would do so at the expense of his entire theory of knowledge. In defending this further claim, he points to the following passage in which Peirce seems clearly to insist that the referent of every perceptual judgement must be an individual.

> If I had denied that every perceptual judgement refers, as to its subject, to a singular, and that singular actually reacting upon the mind in forming the judgement, actually reacting too upon the

mind in interpreting the judgement, I should have uttered an absurdity. (5.152)

In short, Riley claims that unless the integrity of the individual is maintained, both Peirce's metaphysics and his epistemology appear inconsistent.

Having said this much, Riley suggests that Boler's mistake is grounded in his assumption that Secondness and Thirdness "are not only irreducible, but also separable." To take these categories as being separate in any but a highly abstract and formal sense, Riley claims, is to do violence to Peirce's realism and his view of individuals. Since the categories are introduced in the context of phenomenology, or of what Peirce sometimes calls "phaneroscopy," they must be understood as elements or aspects of the "phaneron." As such, they are never in fact isolated from one another, but are rather "inextricably mixed together" wherever they appear. It is only possible to conceive of them as separate after having performed the process of abstraction which Peirce calls "prescission." Inasmuch as Boler appears to neglect this fundamental principle of Peirce's categories, Riley holds that his analysis of the place of the individual in Peirce is at the very least "suspect."

Riley suggests that a more accurate interpretation of the relation of the individual to the universal in Peirce can be made in terms of a "rule-model." That is, the universal is a part of the individual in the sense of governing or regulating it.

> . . . to say that the general is a part of the individual would be a quaint way of saying that certain rules justify a given interpretation of a person's behavior or that an appeal to certain regularities and norms constitute the determination of an object's classification or an action's success.[12]

And he believes that with this interpretation, he at once avoids the mistake of which he accuses Boler, and presents a way in which Peirce can deny the principle of contraction while maintaining that the universal is a part of the individual.

§3

There are two reasons for having undertaken the foregoing discussion of the positions of Boler and Riley: first, they forcefully present opposing views of the relation between the individual and the universal in Peirce, and second, I believe that, however disparate their views, they share that fundamental misinterpretation of the structure of Peirce's categories mentioned in the first section.

It should be clear enough that I am in agreement with Riley's argument against Boler to the extent that he affirms the importance of the individual for Peirce. It is certainly true that unless we are willing to hold that Peirce is seriously inconsistent in his thinking — or, perhaps, endorse the notion that there are two, three, or some indefinite number of Peirces — the individual plays an integral role in his metaphysics. Otherwise, Peirce must appear as an Hegelian, albeit a rather unsystematic one, and that, as we have seen, is something that he consistently denied. However, in his eagerness to maintain and support the position of the individual in Peirce, Riley suggests a view which is, I think, just as incompatible with Peirce's own as is Boler's. On his interpretation, it is the universal which fades into the background as the individual comes to the fore.

While Riley's immediate concern is to emphasize the significance of the individual, in order to assess the merit of his position as a whole, we must also attend to the implicit status which he assigns to the universal. Peirce's understanding of the universal would, on Riley's interpretation, be reducible to a "body of rules, regularities, or norms, not the Common Nature of Scotus' metaphysics." And as such, the universal seems to be confined to what we might call the "linguistic" as opposed to the "real" order. Generals appear to be *merely* linguistic items which develop out of our attempts to describe individuals. We adopt rules, notice regularities, and apply norms in rendering intelligible our encounters with individuals. However, if we are to understand universals in this way, that is as mere constituents of our cognitive experience of individuals, it is difficult to see how they could sustain any independence from that experience.

And that universals are independent of any particular knowing relation, of "what you or I might think," is a position which Peirce repeatedly asserts. Universals, he says in several places, are "real facts," which is presumably to say that they have an independent reality. Consider, for example, his claim that

> Generality is, indeed, an indispensible ingredient of reality; for mere individual existence or actuality without any regularity whatever is a nullity. Chaos is pure nothing. (5.431)

Or again, in the fourth lecture of the series he delivered at Harvard in the spring of 1903, he argues that "Thirdness is operative in Nature." Proposing to let a stone fall from his hand to the floor, he said:

> It would be quite absurd to say that I could be enabled to know how events are going to be determined over which I can exercise no more control than I shall be able to exercise over this stone after it shall have left my hand, that I can so peer into the future merely on the strength of any acquaintance with any pure fiction. (5.94)

Universality, or law, is a structure of the world which is encountered by us; as such, it cannot be some facet of our experience of the world. It is, for Peirce, very much a part of the real order.

Now the characterization of universals implied in Riley's account is something quite different from this. Generals, he says, "govern but are not in individuals."[13] And he apparently means by this that universals are nothing more than the rules and regularities which we "apply" to individuals or which we "adopt" in describing the *manner* in which individuals act. In other words, our application of rules, our adoption of norms, seems to involve an active constitution of generals. But if this is the case, the independence which Peirce asserts for the reality of the universal must fall away. Riley's view appears to be a form of nominalism, which, as we have seen, was entirely unacceptable to Peirce.

Moreover, on this account, the individual appears as a bare particular. It is *merely* a brute fact which in reacting gives rise to the possibility of descriptions of certain kinds. But these descriptions must be confined to the individual's manner of reaction, and can tell us nothing of the individual *per se*. Universals, as characterized by Riley, may be able to "surround" the individual (relate to it as a cluster of relevant rules), and in this sense could define it negatively, but since they can never really be a part of the individual, it must remain entirely outside our cognitive experience. And if this is the case, Riley has fallen into the Kantian dilemma of asserting the existence of something to which he has already denied himself access.

It seems that for Riley individuals are encountered as brute centers of force, and that universals are generated as a result of our attempts to take account of such encounters. But the individual and the general remain separate from one another. Individuals exist as things altogether independent of our experience, and universals, conversely, appear to be entirely dependent upon the same experience. And to the extent that Riley is willing to identify individuals with Secondness, and universals with Thirdness, his characterization of the relation between the two results in an irreconcilable breach between Peirce's categories of phenomenological experience. The former is understood to be a part of the real order, while the latter is confined to the linguistic order.

For Riley, to say that the universal is part of the individual is nothing more than to say that "such-and-such regularities can be ascribed to x," or "x appears to conform to such-and-such rules or laws."[14] Here, the universal appears to be at most something abstracted from the character and activities of the individual. Rather than being an "indispensable ingredient of reality," as Peirce insists it must be, the universal seems to be something coincidentally generated by the actions or qualities of this or that individual, which is itself a bare unintelligible particular. Or, to put this objection in the terms of the "sheriff analogy" mentioned in the first chapter, Riley seems to make the laws dependent upon the sheriff's decision to execute them. To be sure, the laws would have little effect or importance without the

the existence of the sheriff, but they cannot be, for Peirce in any case, either logically or ontologically dependent upon his existence. Riley's universal is not really a part of the individual, but rather something which can at most supply the context within which the individual acts. If Boler errs on the side of idealism, Riley seems to fall into what Peirce might have called the nominalistic trap.

But a more significant objection might be raised against both Boler and Riley. When they refer to the categories in their discussions, they both seem to take it for granted that if Thirdness is equivalent to the universal, Secondness is equivalent to the individual. Thus, they are both ready to translate the claims that they make concerning the relation between the universal and the individual into claims about Thirdness and Secondness.

Though it is only in terms of the categories that Peirce's position on the relation of the universal to the individual can be properly understood, it is a serious mistake to confound Secondness with the individual. At one point in his paper, Riley holds that Boler would have done better to keep in mind the fact that the categories are most importantly developed in terms of Peirce's phenomenology. He makes this point in objecting that Boler's thesis presupposes an illegitimate separation of Secondness and Thirdness. And so far, his objection is well-founded. However, Riley does not develop the full implications of this objection. That is, we must always bear in mind that the categories are presented as *elements* or *aspects* of phenomena. They are not themselves phenomena in Peirce's sense of the term, but things which characterize or "belong to" phenomena. Further, one category never appears without the others; they are present everywhere, and always together.

> The universal categories belong to every phenomenon, one being perhaps more prominent in one aspect of that phenomenon than another, but all of them belonging to every phenomenon. (5.43)

Seconds, then, must be understood as aspects of phenomena. They appear not as individuals *per se*, but as the aspect of individuality which characterizes every phenomenon. That is,

Secondness refers not to an individual, but to individuality, to a facet of a phenomenon as it is present to us. When we speak of the Secondness of Socrates, for example, we are not referring to the individual called "Socrates," but to that aspect of his being as a phenomenon which makes him individual.

The Secondness of a phenomenon can be most broadly described in terms of two characters which the phenomenon has insofar as it is individual. First, it has a mode of being "independent of any quality or determination whatsoever." (1.434) In its Secondness, the phenomenon is present to us as *other*, as something sheerly self-assertive. Second, in its individuality, the phenomenon is "determinate in regard to every possibility or quality, either as possessing it or not possessing it." (1.434)

There may appear at first to be a certain inconsistency in this dual characterization of individuality. To insist on the one hand that whatever is individual must be entirely independent of any determination whatsoever, and on the other that it is "entirely determinate" with regard to every quality could be interpreted as being at the very least problematic. And unfortunately, Peirce does little to explicate his point. However, the apparent inconsistency is avoided if we take Peirce to mean that the individual character of a thing is independent of any *external* determination. It is independent of such determination precisely because it is in itself wholly determinate. The individuality of a phenomenon is what it is simply in being not anything else. It does not rely upon any sort of external definition—even though such might be offered — and refuses all mediation.

Secondness renders a phenomenon both independent of any external determination, and wholly determinate in itself at any given moment. It is that about a phenomenon which lends to it its individuality: it is a "thisness or thatness." We might say with respect to Socrates that it is his "Socratesness," that which makes him identifiable as Socrates and no other. Again, Secondness is that facet of Socrates the phenomenon, the individual, which is entirely discrete and self-contained. My point, simply put, is this: if we are to speak of the individual in Peirce's system, we must speak of a phenomenon, and not of the category of Secondness. For Secondness is better understood as the *ground* of the individuality of the phenomenon, as that which makes it individual.

Now this interpretation of Peirce's individual sheds a rather different light upon the question of its relation to the universal. Universality, or Thirdness, is as much a part of the individual as is Secondness. That is, it is an aspect of its being as a phenomenon, a facet of the way in which the individual phenomenon appears to, or is encountered by, the observer. The laws to which a phenomenon conforms, the general characteristics and habits which it exhibits when taken together form that aspect or element of the phenomenon which Peirce calls Thirdness. And these laws, habits, etc., are an integral part of the phenomenon itself; they are, in a manner of speaking, very much "in" it. They compose that part of any phenomenon which renders it cognitively accessible to us.

Peirce says at one point that "for the realist, things do not need reasons, they *are* reasons." (4.36) Here he is talking about the extent to which his own position is a version of scholastic realism, and in order to make this claim, he clearly must assume that universals are *in* things. There is something mind-like or reasonable about any given thing (or, at least about any "thing" which we can know), and it is in terms of that quality or aspect that we are able to interpret it. But this certainly need not be taken to mean that these "things" are *only* reasons, only mind-like structures which admit of a reduction to particular concatenations of universals. For, as phenomena, — and I am assuming that the term 'things' as used above can legitimately be identified with 'phenomena' — they must also exhibit Secondness. Contrary to Hegel, they must appear as brute facts which are irreducible. Considered in terms of that aspect of their being which presents itself to us as "brute fact," they simply are not subject to interpretation. To attempt to interpret this facet or aspect would be to make the mistake of assuming that Secondness can be dissolved into Thirdness; it could result in nothing more than a fruitless effort to mediate that which is by nature immediate.

§4

In speaking of Peirce's categories and their relation to what we might call the "Peircean individual" I have been relying implicitly upon a distinction between individuals and individuality. Since this distinction is crucial to the development of a model for an account of the individual, I should like to turn now to a more direct discussion of the relation between the individual and individuality in Peirce. Though Peirce does speak of the latter, he says little if anything of the individual itself. That is, while he concerns himself with that aspect of phenomena which we may call individuality, or Secondness, he never explicitly characterizes the things to which that aspect obtains. However, I think that it is possible, given what he does say, to construct at least a sketch of what a Peircean individual might be.

As I have already suggested, I think it is most reasonable to begin by holding that for Peirce an individual must be a phenomenon. As such, it is something which can be described in terms of the phenomenological categories we have been discussing. Moreover, the phenomenon is apparently to be understood as that which manifests these categories. For the categories appear to be something more than descriptive tools; that is, they are not to be taken only as broad classifications in terms of which we come to know phenomena. Rather, they are characteristic both of the way in which we know phenomena, and of the phenomena themselves. As Peirce has it, the categories "belong to" phenomena. That is, they are "in" phenomena in some sense and not merely ascribed to them. The point that I am trying to make here is that it is important not to misunderstand the categories by taking them to be "interpretations" of phenomena. Interpretation is a task which is specifically assigned to *one* of the categories: Thirdness. And even Thirdness, from Peirce's point of view, is not some external classification in terms of which phenomena are grouped, but an essential mode of being attached to every phenomenon to the extent that it enters our experience as something which is cognitively accessible.

Secondness, likewise, stands apart from the usual connotations attached to the term 'category' inasmuch as it is meant to describe another of the essential features of the phenomenon: its ability to stand apart from the fabric of mediated relations — or Thirdness — as something undeniably *other*. It is an "essential feature" in the sense of being another of the modes of being which the phenomenon exhibits; it is that about the phenomenon in terms of which it appears as a thing determined in and of itself.

Now if we take the "Peircean individual" to be a phenomenon, it is possible to describe it as displaying the characters of both Secondness and Thirdness, of both individuality and universality. It may at first seem gratuitous to point to the fact that every individual must exhibit a facet which we can call individuality. But individuality, or what Peirce refers to as Secondness, is precisely that part of our experience which Hegel ignores and which is in general relegated to a position of insignificance by the idealistic branch of the western tradition. To say that an individual possesses individuality does not mean simply that it is unique, that it can be distinguished from other things in terms of some general feature which it evinces. Uniqueness is, after all, only one universal among many which can be appropriately applied to some things and not to others. It is just this sort of reasoning which led Hegel to claim that in being a "one" any individual thing establishes its identity with every other rather than its difference. Individuality cannot be understood to be one universal among others, for no universal, given the triadic structure of universals, could stand as the ground of that infinite resistance with which we meet in any encounter with individuals. And it must be to this ground that we refer when we speak of a thing's individuality.

Consider a particular human individual. (Though this description might be taken up in terms of any individual, it can perhaps be most vividly represented in human terms.) After we have stripped away or reduced all of the generals by which we would usually characterize this individual, there remains a certain residue which refuses any further reduction. It is that facet of the individual which presents itself to us as wholly other. And considered in terms of this facet, the individual stands only in external relation to the things around him. Individuality as an aspect of his being is something entirely discrete; it appears to ground itself. Whatever relations it may have to other things are purely incidental. It is this facet's manner of being starkly self-contained that gives rise to the brute resistance we experience when we meet the individual. We might say figuratively that Secondness or individuality is that aspect of the individual which turns in upon itself; it seems to have a kind of self-sustaining vitality which refuses the discursive interpretations of Thirdness.

A problem arises as soon as one tries to offer this sort of description: it seems impossible to avoid getting entangled in a sort of linguistic trap. While insisting that individuality cannot be reduced to any concatenation of universals, however peculiar, one is nevertheless forced to use universals in the very statement that universals are inappropriate here. Further, individuality must be an aspect common to all individuals, and as such appears to be itself a universal. Thus, we must bear in mind that though it is convenient to use the term, 'individuality' of itself is no more than an empty abstraction. Each individual can be characterized by 'individuality,' or in Peirce's terms, exhibits Secondness, but the very nature of that aspect of its being denies the possibility of being considered as an instance of a universal. Instances are never discrete and self-contained; they stand by nature in internal and necessary relation to one another.

When we use the term 'individuality' to refer to existent individuals, then, we refer not to a class or a set, but to a *collection of discrete beings.* And it is as a term significant only insofar as individuals actually exist. Presumably, this is one of the reasons that Peirce consistently allies Secondness with existence. It is a category which is meaningful only insofar as it describes the actions and reactions, or what Peirce sometimes calls the "struggle," of individual, existing things. Our recognition of individuality arises out of the immediate experience of brute facts, those facts which Descartes described as being simply beyond our control. One cannot think an umbrella shut in a strong wind any more than he can use a theory of nutrition to convince a child that he should eat his spinach. No more will a theoretical rejection of the law of gravity keep a heavy object from falling. To insist upon the existence of individuals is in one sense simply to assert, on the basis of the most common experiences, the existence of radical otherness. And, here, otherness is to be understood not as relative difference, but as opposition *per se.* Relative differences can be subsumed by mediatory frameworks as readily as similarities, but opposition in and of itself, that equally constant aspect of our experience, remains by nature entirely distinct from such frameworks. Peirce's category of Secondness represents an attempt to take account of it.

Now just as the individual phenomenon, the "Peircean individual," exhibits the character of individuality or Secondness, so is it characterized by a certain universality: Thirdness is an equally essential ingredient of the phenomenon. It appears in various guises: participation in laws, habit-taking so-called, and more simply, in any general characteristic. Considered in terms of his Thirdness or universality, the human individual, for example, is necessarily a part of a community. For the universals which he exhibits transcend his instancing of them, and form the fabric of the community. Though the participation of the individual in a law is not essential to the reality of the law, it is an essential aspect of the being of the individual as a phenomenon. The various appearances which the individual phenomenon takes on as a member of a community, the laws and habits by which he can be characterized are part and parcel of the meaning of the phenomenon and therefore of its being. It must be this that Peirce intends when he says that "things *are* reasons," and that man is a "sign."

By virtue of its Thirdness, the phenomenon participates in a network of interpretation and of "interpretants." With respect to this aspect of its being, it exhibits and is constituted by what is ideal, mind-or law-like. The phenomenon, in its universality, *is* law. But since its individuality, or Secondness, is likewise an essential aspect of its being — here I should prefer to say one of its "modes" of being — it can never be thought of as reducible to law. For it is also forcefully real, in the sense of being a "brute fact." Being a phenomenon, then, entails being both real and ideal, both individual and universal, both a second and a third.

Perhaps this point can be more clearly stated if we return for a moment to the consideration of a human individual. I have been interpreting Peirce's notion of Thirdness to refer to those general characteristics which we commonly use in describing such an individual. While these characteristics vary widely in depth and scope, we might choose as examples political and psychological descriptions. Considered as a member of any political community, one can be described in terms of a series of principles — here, legal ones — which are taken to apply to anyone who participates in the community. Take, for example, the notion of "human rights" as it appears in our own society. To be sure, this notion is interpreted in different ways by various political systems, but there is at least some sense in which they all share a common understanding of the idea. In any case, I am not interested here in taking a political position of one kind or another, but rather in pointing to the way in which these rights could be interpreted on the Peircean model. When we say that an American citizen has, say, the right to liberty, we describe him in such a way that he is drawn into an extremely complex network of laws. And it is in terms of these laws that he is related both to other individuals and to society considered as a whole.

Given such a set of laws, it becomes possible for others and for the individual himself to form certain expectations regarding the political dimensions of his world. And these expectations are finally translated into the sorts of boundaries (in this case, the political restrictions, privileges, etc.) which serve to define and structure at least one aspect of the experience of the entire society. In fact, it can make sense to refer to a group of individuals as a society only insofar as they are prepared to endorse some such network of laws. But once a network of this kind is established, it assumes an active role in the constitution of the individuals which participate in it. While the laws can exist only so long as the members of the society continue to endorse them, the existence of a group of individuals *qua* members of a society is equally dependent upon the laws. (Surely it is to this that Socrates refers when he describes the laws of Athens as his "parents and teachers." Or, one might think of the way in which the average American citizen is inclined to speak of himself and others as "having" rights.)

The point here is simply that laws are not merely incidental to the being of the individual. They constitute an essential aspect of what he is, and that as much from the individual's own point of view as from external ones. At the same time, however, the individual is capable of responding to laws in a variety of ways. While he can actively endorse them, he can as easily neglect or refuse them. And to the extent that he also displays this capacity, he can never be completely defined in terms of a set of laws — even if we restrict the definition to the political dimension of his experience. There is always at least this sense in which he stands apart from, and perhaps even over against laws. The "right to liberty," for example, is sometimes refused by individuals, and at other times "taken away" from them. When we describe an individual as a member of a society, we point at once to his participation in a set of laws and to his ability to accept or reject them. In short, we point to the dimension of universality which characterizes him, and to the individuality which his very existence presupposes.

The same point might be made in terms of psychological descriptions. Consider the claims made by those who continue to be attracted to the neuroses and psychoses of the Freudian landscape. Emotional difficulties of various kinds are condensed into a group of neatly defined categories in such a way that it becomes possible to identify individuals as paranoids, schizophrenics, and so on. While I am personally inclined to reject Freud's psychology as utter nonsense, I have been forced to recognize the power which his categories have assumed vis-à-vis the self-definition of many of the people I meet. Let me offer an extreme example. A bright and attractive freshman came to my office not long ago to explain having dropped out of a course in the middle of the term. She said that she had become so anxious that she could no longer bring herself either to attend classes or to study. I asked her what the problem seemed to be, and it turned out that her psychologist had told her that she was likely to *inherit* her father's "manic-depression." She was terrified. This particular category had become for her something more than an abstraction; she was beginning to define herself in terms of it and, as a result, seemed to me to be on the verge of permitting a large part of her general experience to be shaped by it. It is perhaps in this way that such categories too often take on the character of self-fulfilling prophecies.

Now while I am hardly qualified to offer a clinical opinion about this, it did strike me at the time as an instance of a category in the process of becoming what Peirce might have called a "real fact." That is, something that is on the face of it merely a general description had entered forcefully into the immediate experience of an individual, and had, as a result, become quite real. It was real for her in the sense that it had importantly altered her view of the world and her place in it; real for those around her to the extent that it reshaped their various relationships with her. But all of this considered, surely even the most avid Freudian would stop short of claiming that the girl had become identical with "manic-depression." For categories of this sort, however significant they might become in both a theoretical and a practical sense, can never completely circumscribe an individual. They can at most describe a certain facet of the individual's being: a way of standing in mediated relation to others which makes classification possible. This is not to say that there is another aspect of the individual which is somehow more fundamental, but simply that there are other aspects. In the case at hand, for example, one can easily imagine circumstances where the individual could lead herself or be led to put aside her anxiety. In fact, if she did not in some sense stand apart from this categorical description, the only possible response to her predicament would be despair.

Nor is it necessary to focus upon unusual examples to make this point. We need only think of the times when we have been surprised by something that a close friend has said or done in order to recognize the limits of categorical description. And, on the other hand, the importance of this sort of description becomes evident whenever we try to characterize the same friend for someone outside his or her acquaintance.

In short, the universals which we use in attempting to describe an individual are always necessary but never adequate. And they seem to be inadequate, not in the sense that some more complete set might be supplied, but rather in that there is something about the individual which denies categorization. There is an aspect of its being which remains recalcitrant in the face of the mediation which laws provide. I think that Peirce intends to direct our attention to this recalcitrance when he speaks of "brute fact" and the "this-ness or that-ness" of things. Secondness, the category of struggle and opposition, provides a place in the midst of a discursive account for this aspect of our experience. And, *given the equal significance which Peirce attaches to Thirdness,* it need not do so at the expense of reducing idealism to nominalism.

If we take the world to be made up out of the kind of phenomenal individuals sketched above, some of the traditional problems surrounding the relation of the universal to the individual simply fall away. When universality and individuality are understood as categories of relations in which individuals stand to one another, it is no longer necessary to ask how or why the universal can be a "part" of the individual. For universals, on this account, do not appear as reified structures which are by nature dirempt from the individual. They enter our experience as more or less useful descriptions of the network of mediated relations in which every individual — to the extent that it is or can become intelligible — must stand to whatever it is not. And, inasmuch as no such network is capable of circumscribing the palpable resistance which individuals always present when we try to reduce them to "instances" of universals, a satisfactory description of experience must also include the Second category of relation: the category or mode of being which I have called "individuality."

As I suggested earlier in this chapter, it seems to me that Peirce offers a way of consolidating the conflicts which arise in the relation between realism and idealism. The notion of the phenomenal individual can be used as a point of departure in the development of what might be called a descriptive metaphysics. Having asserted that universality and individuality inhere in phenomena in equally significant ways, the task of such a metaphysics is to go on to describe the relations which obtain between these two facets of phenomena. If we are to move beyond Hegel, as Peirce attempted to do, it is necessary to take account of both the "ideal" and the "real" as essential aspects of our experience. And when they are drawn together as distinguishable—albeit inseparable — aspects of the individual, one need not be taken to overwhelm the other, or to be somehow a more fundamental structure in the world. Both act to colour and shape our experience of the world as well as our consciousness of ourselves.

The thorough development of such a metaphysics is a project which I assume will take years to complete. I think that the Peircean model offers a solid foundation, but it is at the same time only a skeletal framework which lacks the flesh and blood of a complete account. While we can turn to Hegel for a forceful and full-bodied account of the universal in our experience, there is no one in the philosophical tradition who presents an equally adequate account of individuality. I have tried to show how Peirce's metaphysics can be interpreted to provide a logical space for such an account, but Peirce offers only hints concerning the structure of the category which fills that space. This is the case not least because the dyadic nature of individuality seems to defy conventionally discursive categorization. As a result, a new sort of philosophical language must be developed if we are ever successfully to present an account of individuality within a broader metaphysical structure. I am not prepared to claim that I have this language ready at hand any more than the account which I think it will make possible. However, in the concluding chapter, I shall try to offer some suggestions about the direction which I think we must take toward the development of both.

Chapter 4
Toward A New Beginning:
Art, Philosophy, and Individuality

Where the meaningful law of a heaven used to
arch, with the spindle of necessity hanging
from its bright vault, the meaningless,
tyrannical power of the planets now holds sway.

Martin Buber

T HE PHILOSOPHER INEVITABLY attempts to deal with metaphysical issues in structural terms which seem to deny
the irreducible dimension of individuality present in direct experience. But this is not to say that individuality cannot
be dealt with in philosophical terms. As I suggested in the last
chapter, it is simply necessary that philosophy generate a language capable of taking account of this other aspect of our
experience. In this final chapter, I should like to offer some
suggestions concerning the direction in which I think such a
language must develop.

Individuality is neither a quality nor a category; it is a mode
of being. To characterize a thing as an individual is to point to
its participation in a singular relation to what it is not. And it
is to this relation that we must attend if we are to develop a
philosophical language which can adequately articulate the force
and significance of the individual in general experience. While
it evolves out of resistance and denial, this relation must nevertheless be characterized by a certain reciprocity inasmuch as it
is always dyadic. That is, when we say that something is individual, we point to a way in which it stands apart from that
which it is not, but at the same time seem to draw it into relation
with whatever is external to it. Since this relation is an unmediated one, it is different in structure from conventional clas-

75

sification. Nevertheless, it is a relation, and as such, it is something which is reflectively accessible at least to the extent that we can describe its logical structure.

In the last chapter, I tried to show how Peirce can be seen to offer a model in terms of which this relation can be brought into the framework of a discursive account. The importance of the dyad, and its place in a description of experience become clear when we take the phenomenal individual as a fundamental term. The problem which confronts us, however, is how we might begin to characterize that part of our experience which cannot be subsumed by the mediatory frameworks of discursive thought traditionally defined. Having already established the logical constitution of this aspect of experience, it seems to me that we must look outside the boundaries of conventional philosophical discourse for solutions.

As an altogether different medium of human expression, art might hold out the key. Art is as much an attempt to speak to our experience as is philosophy, but the focus of art is significantly different. Where the philosophical tradition has focused upon the universal, art directs our attention to the individual. In what follows, I shall undertake a discussion of the relation between art and philosophy in an attempt to discover what it is about art which allows it the sort of access to the individual which seems to elude traditional philosophical accounts. Let me begin by putting the following question: how can art be distinguished from philosophy, and how can this distinction help us understand the notion of individuality and the relationship between the universal and the individual dimensions of our experience?

A discussion of this sort is made difficult not least by the fact that the task of differentiation is properly a philosophical one. The artist simply need not concern himself with it. And when the philosopher does so, he brings with him a philosophical style and method, and almost always ends in producing an account of art which makes it appear to be merely a different kind of philosophy. In approaching art as something which can be adequately described in terms of a series of universals, he attempts to analyze it in much the same way as one might analyze a philosophical system. But art does not deal primarily with the universal; it focuses rather upon the individual, upon that which is discrete and wholly self-contained. An object of art is an individual, and it is one in a way in which no philosophical system, however unique and carefully integrated, can be.

Since I am using the terms 'individual' and 'individuality' here in the sense described in the last chapter, it might be well to turn first to a brief characterization of the way in which I understand them to apply to art. What does it mean to hold that the work of art is an individual? I have already suggested that the individual is something discrete and self-contained. That is, it is a whole. Now to say that the work of art considered as an individual appears to be a *whole* is not merely to say that it is internally coherent. It certainly means at least this, but at the same time it is my intention to point to the manner or mode of being exhibited by the work. Consider, for example, any one of Cézanne's later views of Mont St.-Victoire. Blues, yellows, greens, join together vibrantly to form a valley which could be a village, and a mountain which seems just to hesitate before becoming the sky. There is activity here, and it is an activity that we confront in the picture itself—not one, that is to say, merely imputed to it by the viewer. Moreover, this dynamic character of the painting, the activity which we discover in it, is thoroughly self-referential. The picture is active, it bodies forth a certain mode of being, not in referring to something outside itself, but rather in turning back upon itself to refer to and sustain its *own* ontological landscape. In other words, we can say that the painting is actively engaged in individuating itself.

Now this facet of the work of art must remain, at least in one sense, cognitively opaque to us. We cannot "know" it in the common philosophical sense of the term. That is, the self-individuating character of the work cannot be penetrated by means of a discursive account. One can, at best, attempt to point to this character of art in such a way that its significance and force are not allowed to dissolve in the midst of an otherwise systematic discussion. Nevertheless, this facet of the work of art is certainly an undeniable feature of our experience of it. It is precisely this character which is the seat of the power or the life, if you like, which we experience when we are confronted by a masterpiece. A thoroughly insistent self-identity lies at the very center of the work, and it is translated into our experience as the exhilaration and even perhaps the threat which we know when we stand before it. It is that in the work of art which we experience as ineluctably *other.* Every good work of art, in exhibiting this facet of its being, declares itself to be independent of external determination. We encounter it as something capable of grounding itself. It supports and sustains itself as a world richly textured, related only coincidentally to what we can call *the* world, or what contemporary phenomenologists have called the intersubjective world.

Now just as in the case of the Peircean phenomenon, in claiming that an object of art is an individual, I do not mean to deny that it has to do with the universal, that there are universals which are manifested by it, and others which can be appropriately ascribed to it. For obviously, unless the universal were present in objects of art, it would be impossible to make *any* cognitively accessible statements about them. The point is rather that no work of art can be exhaustively characterized by a series of universals — even an infinite series — which are either discovered within it or applied to it externally. This becomes clear, for example, when we think of the characters of a play. After we have said as much of Hamlet as can possibly be said, there remains a stubborn and palpable residue which *is* Hamlet. And it is to this residue that I mean to point in saying that he is an individual. All of the universals by which he can be characterized are shot through with his individuality, an individuality which remains perfectly irreducible to a series of generals, no matter how complete.

Nevertheless, we can and do speak of Hamlet in terms of his universal characteristics. His condition is in many ways representative of the human condition in general. His indecisiveness, his complex relations with his parents and with Ophelia can be said both to echo and in some sense to typify similar general structures in a world beyond the contours of the play. Although we are confronted in our experience of Hamlet by a discrete individual, one who exhibits the mode of being I have called 'individuality,' we notice at the same time that this individual evinces a wide range of universal characters. He is not strictly or barely individual, but participates simultaneously in a certain universality. And yet each of the universals in terms of which we can legitimately characterize Hamlet is coloured by that individuality to which I have already attempted to point. There is a quality that might be called "Hamletness" which lingers about each of the general features ascribable to Hamlet. He is indecisive in a way that only Hamlet could be, though indecision itself is certainly a common enough feature of human character.

Similarly, to return to the Cézanne picture, we recognize that while the colours, shapes, textures and lines of the painting are in fact general features, they take on a peculiar aspect when they are seen as parts of this particular painting. The blue of the sky is a colour which we find not only in other paintings, but often in the sky itself. It reaches beyond the painting to participate in a universal structure of an intersubjective world, and yet, as a part of the painting, it participates in the mode of individuality which we recognize in the painting as a whole. It remains universal while coming to be at the same time individuated. In other words, the blue which Cézanne used, as being something integrated into this *particular* whole, comes to be something more than it was before such an integration: more in that it is not only an instance of a universal, a blue splotch, but also participant in a relation unavailable to universals *qua* universals. It stands in a sense, over against the universal we call blue, over against itself. It is the blue of *this* sky, the sky of *this* picture, and while it might be a colour which one could meet elsewhere, it becomes rich and meaningful as a result of its integral place in the construction of this picture. The mode of individuality is made available to it only insofar as it participates in the painting.

A philosophical system, traditionally defined, can never exhibit this sort of individuality. As an attempt to give a discursive account of what is, it cannot be an individual. For it is precisely a series of universals, and is an individual only in the sense of being distinguishable from other such series. When we call it individual, what we must mean is simply that it is unique, that the particular series of universals which it employs or its peculiar concatenation of them is like that of no other system. But to attribute uniqueness to something, as we have seen, amounts in fact only to ascribing another general feature to it. It is not to claim for it that sort of individuality which can be evinced by a work of art.

Wallace Stevens is perhaps more successful in making this point metaphorically. In "An Ordinary Evening in New Haven," Professor Eucalyptus says,

> The search
> For reality is as momentous as
> The search for god. It is the philosopher's search
> For an interior made exterior
> And the poet's search for the same exterior made
> Interior: breathless things broodingly abreath
>
> With the inhalations of original cold
> And of original earliness.

Stevens seems to point here to both a similarity and a difference in the tasks undertaken by the philosopher and the artist. To the extent that both are involved in what he calls the "search for reality," philosophy and art join together in the movement toward a single τέλος. Each may be seen to develop as an attempt to articulate the most important aspects of our experience. But even if there is a sense in which they share a common goal, the philosopher and the artist can be distinguished from one another in terms of their various ways of understanding the relation between that end and its beginning. In both cases, beginnings and ends are interwoven inasmuch as any intelligible development demands such a relation. But where the artist understands his "end" to be the articulation of the concrete range of immediate possibility inherent in his beginning, the philosopher insists that the most significant aspect of *his* beginning is that which is structured in accord with an already determinately articulated end. As a result, the character of their speech differs strikingly. The philosopher speaks systematically; that is, his speech is thoroughly dependent upon that which is external to it. It is, and properly holds itself to be, responsible to a truth which is not merely its own. In other words, he is forced to take account of and to employ the categorical structures in terms of which discursive thought becomes generally accessible. The artist, on the other hand, in focusing upon the immediate and irreducible dimension of experience, produces a mode of expression capable of creating and sustaining its own truth. His speech is always the "exterior made interior"; always a beginning which insists upon its place as a new moment completely independent of whatever pasts and futures we might try to impose upon it. As such it is a speech capable of embodying and presenting the sort of individuals discussed above.

The distinction I have tried to draw can be made in terms of what might be called the different directionalities of art and philosophy. There is a sense in which both are circular; but while philosophy is always a beginning in search of an end, art returns upon itself as an end attempting to express its beginning. Think again of Hegel's claim that "the line of scientific advance becomes a circle." His dialectic is animated by an attempt to articulate a conceptual framework complex and rich enough to reconcile the conflict apparent in its first moment. When he finally presents this reconciliation in the form of the Absolute Idea, he asserts that the end he has discovered is not *an* end, but *the* end. It is that in the sense that it has entirely subsumed its beginning; his system has taken that beginning up into itself in such a way that it can no longer be logically distinguished from the end which it seems to demand. The line has in fact become a circle inasmuch as, from the perspective of Absolute Knowledge, every point is both beginning and end. That is, the end has returned to its beginning, but its structure has become so thoroughly mediated in the process that it can only attend to that aspect of its beginning which is consonant with a particular mode of reflective development. No conflict has been resolved: Hegel has simply chosen one of the paths which his beginning makes possible, and then reinterpreted that beginning in terms of the framework which is a necessary issue of his original choice. But the choice itself is not one which is, as Hegel would have it, demanded by reason; it is one among several which he might have made. In saying this, I do not mean to hold that his return to and redefinition of his beginning is in itself illegitimate. It only becomes so when he refuses to recognize the importance of the beginning *qua* beginning. The contours of that first moment can never be wholly definite, and while we must construct boundaries in the attempt to make it reflectively accessible, we must continually remind ourselves of the artificial character of those boundaries. Without a recognition of this, philosophical advance is impossible.

In emphasizing the universal dimension of our experience, philosophy has always brought its beginning into a necessary relation with its end. That is, the end is seen to return to its beginning as a more complete articulation of the mediated structure implicitly or potentially evident in the first moment. It is this that accounts for Hegel's insistence that the line of scientific advance must ultimately become a circle. Now there is also a sense in which artistic advance involves a return to its beginning. However, this return is constituted not by an attempt to redefine the beginning in terms of its end, but rather by a desire to come to a more complete understanding of the end in the light of the infinite complexity of its beginning. As I have emphasized already in the discussion of Peirce's objection to Hegel, the dimension of our experience which can be characterized as opposition or struggle is as essential to a complete account of phenomena as are the universal categories of Hegel's system. And it is to this dimension of experience that the work of art attempts to return. It is an expression of a beginning that might give rise to a broad range of ends, and which, as a result, can never be completely defined by any one of them.

As a concrete illustration of this, consider the development of Cézanne's views of Mont St.-Victoire. Merleau-Ponty once said of Cézanne that he was attempting to paint a "primordial world," the world, that is, which stands underneath and to both sides of the world which we describe in terms of scientific categories. To the extent that Cézanne was trying to give us access to such a world, I think we can understand his work to represent a kind of return quite different from that undertaken by philosophy. During the thirty years that he spent painting the mountain and quarry over and over again, he seems to have been working toward an articulation of what might be called his "original" experience of the landscape. The earliest pictures are essentially representational accounts of a carefully defined landscape. Of course, even in these, one finds a masterly use of colour, texture, and shape which redefines ordinary notions of space. But it is nevertheless clear to the viewer that he is looking at a mountain covered with vegetation, railroad trestles and so forth. He is confronted by a landscape, that is to say, which can be easily recognized and characterized in terms of a series of definite categories; he sees a mountain which has been structured by and has taken its place in the development of western culture. But where the philosophical system strives toward this sort of definition and integration as its end, Cézanne takes it as his beginning. His art develops not toward but away from definition. The later paintings of the same mountain are made up of stark slashes of colour. Their power is the power of the immediate; the vitality which they exude, the force which one finds in them, is derived at least in part from their ability to stand over against the categories of reflective discourse.

The beginning to which Cézanne returns can never be circumscribed or subsumed by the particular end to which it has given rise. It is rich and full of possibility not because it demands some single end, but because it could give rise to almost any end. (Perhaps it is this that Wallace Stevens means when he says that "reality is the beginning.") The beginning might be described as the sensuous manifold which we hone and pare into our "scientific" experience of the world. And we are drawn to it as an other which in accepting any definition whatever can be bounded by none.

While Cézanne's return to such a beginning is a convenient example, he is by no means the only artist to whom one might point. I think that much of the work of other impressionists and post-impressionists can be described in these terms, as can German expressionism, absurdist theatre, the poetry of Yeats and Stevens, the novels of Marcel Proust, Henry James, Thomas

Mann and William Faulkner. But, as I said at the outset, it is not my intention in these pages to develop a contemporary aesthetic. I mean simply to point to the way in which art functions as a mode of human expression different from philosophical discourse. In understanding its beginning to be structured by the possible rather than the definite, art can give us access to that part of our experience which defies categorical necessity. In the beginning to which Cézanne, for example, leads us, we find not categories, but the ground out of which they arise. One might say that he presents us with a picture of the world which Hegelian dialectic takes as its point of departure. And he does so unabashedly. This is not a world primordially constituted by a subject-object split in search of some sort of mediation; it is simply what it is. Nor is it, in being indefinite, identical with nothingness. It is replete with being, with the life of the immediate, even while it refuses the boundaries of determinate being. And without a constant awareness of such a world, those boundaries become the empty abstractions of a discourse which has lost all touch with its original purpose.

In presenting a mode of access to the immediate, art offers a kind of expression which can take account of individuality without reducing it to the universal categories of philosophical reflection. It is to this character of the work of art that I meant to point earlier in referring to it as a self-contained "whole" or "world." While we can know and describe works of art in terms of their general characteristics, our experience of them always seems much richer than the general descriptions we construct. One discovers this as soon as he tries to discuss the meaning of a poem with an acquaintance who has yet to read it, or the concrete force of a particular picture with someone who has never seen it. The work of art stands in both universal and individual relation to its audience, and can only be fully understood when it is understood as an *individual.* Part of what this means is that there can never be an absolutely complete understanding of the work of art. As an individual, it stands in a kind of relation to what it is not which, in being immediate, is always new. It represents a perceptual beginning inasmuch as its beginning is never confined or constricted by the imposition of some particular end. If we can turn to Hegel for a thorough exposition of the structure of that dimension of our experience which is mediated, we can look to art for an articulate expression of the dimension which is not.

Reflective thought cannot move beyond the Hegelian system until it recognizes and finds a way to incorporate this other mode of human expression. It seems to me that this will be possible if we take what Hegel taught us and return with it to the sort of beginning sought by Cézanne. That is, we must find a way of describing the relation between the logical structure of the Absolute Idea and the palpable immediacy of the ground out of which it arises. Our experience of the world is simultaneously mediate and immediate, and if we are to give a full-bodied account of it, we must mold our speech in such a way that it can take account of both dimensions.

This path entails certain sacrifices, not the least of which is the eschewing of the ideal of the complete account. While logic need not bow to metaphor, it must come to accept it as something other than a bastard son. And a metaphor can never be complete in the way that a perfectly integrated logical system can be. But no more is our experience of the world, an experience constituted as much by beginnings as by ends, ever complete. In fact, as we have seen, the very notion of the complete speech, of some logical schema comprehensive enough to subsume every aspect of experience, has developed simply as a function of one way of characterizing our relation to what we are not. We look back upon our experience, seeking out similarities within difference, ones among the many, reflectively modifying and emasculating the brute recalcitrance of dyadic relation in accord with the demands pre-ordained by our vision of the Whole. Yet no sooner do we seem to succeed in bringing this project to an end than we are driven back to the beginning by a recognition that we stand as creators not only of this newly refined and integrated Whole, but of the project itself.

In our return to the beginning, we are confronted once again by the radically contingent character of the first moment. Here we discover contingency of a sort which cannot be put aside as categorically intelligible in an Hegelian manner. For Hegel, tingency figures in the development of consciousness only to the extent that one path instead of another has in fact been chosen in the progress toward the Absolute. Seen as such, the notion of contingency is quite rightly neglected as relatively insignificant. But this appears reasonable only when we choose to assess the beginning from the point of view of the end. When, on the other hand, we reflectively place ourselves at the beginning, and from that point of view assess the end, the pervasive indeterminacy of our new position reaches out to shatter the apparently absolute determination of that end. No longer understood to be *the* end, it has become simply *an* end as the all-encompassing unity of the Whole, that complete integration of which we were just a moment ago so certain, dissolves into a plurality of wholes, both possible and actual.

Since this plurality can be seen as a collection of individuals, structured as much by resistance and opposition as by mediation, no complete account of it is possible. However, in characterizing the idea of a complete account as an unattainable goal, we need not endorse the notion that there must remain some facet of our experience which lies outside the boundaries of reflective thought and intelligible description. We must simply remold and broaden our understanding of what constitutes intelligible discourse. If we accept as the only model for an intelligible account the one which is the legacy of the western tradition, an account structured by a determinate set of overarching categorical schemata, we must indeed reconcile ourselves to the certainty that there is a part of our experience which is in principle inaccessible. But this is to say something about the structural character of the account, not about experience.

As I have shown in both logical and concrete contexts, there is without doubt a dimension of our contact with the world which because of its fundamental structure stands over and against the categorical description which the philosophical tradition has tried to impose upon it. The radical opposition which enters our experience as dyadic relation, and which provides the ground for the individual dimension of that experience, is by nature indeterminate and as a result refuses such description. But, here again, we have exposed nothing more than the limits of one kind of description, not of description *per se*. In Cézanne's paintings, in Stevens' poetry, we find another sort of description: one which embodies as it gives us access to the very indeterminacy that eludes the categorical account, and which does so intelligibly. For there lies at the very core of metaphorical expression a tension between the determinate and the indeterminate which is drawn into our reflection upon it as we recognize that the meaning of a metaphor can never be completely articulated. It exposes to us the palpable immediacy of beginnings, the irremediable tension between the individual and the universal, as we resonate with its vibrantly originative image of the indeterminate dimension of our experience.

With the culmination of the modern project, we may well have learned as much as can be learned by attempting to understand beginnings in the light of the ends which issue from them. Let us turn our attention now to a reassessment of those ends in the light of their beginnings, and to the generation of a new speech, which in affording us access to the individual as well as the universal, can never be complete.

Notes

Chapter 2

1. G. W. F. Hegel, *Phenomenology of Spirit*, trans. A. V. Miller (Oxford: Oxford University Press, 1977), p. 10. (Cited hereafter as *Phenomenology.*)

2. Ibid., p. 12.

3. G. W. F. Hegel, *Science of Logic*, trans. Johnston and Struthers (New York: Macmillan, 1961), p. 83. (Cited hereafter as *Logic.*)

4. Ibid., p. 83.

5. Ibid., p. 84.

6. *Phenomenology*, p. 58.

7. Ibid., p. 58.

8. Ibid., p. 58.

9. Ibid., p. 59.

10. Ibid., p. 60.

11. Ibid., p. 62.

12. Ibid., p. 65.

13. Ibid., p. 67.

14. Ibid., p. 67.

15. v., e.g., G. W. F. Hegel, *Lectures on the History of Philosophy*, trans. Haldane and Simson (London: Routledge and Kegan Paul, 1955), Vol. II, p. 56.

16. *Sophist* $238C_{10}$.

17. *Sophist* 256E.

18. *Phenomenology*, p. 66.

19. Ibid., p. 69.

20. Ibid., p. 73.

21. Ibid., p. 76.

22. Ibid., p. 143.

23. *Logic*, p. 119.

Chapter 3

1. *Collected Papers of Charles Sanders Peirce*, Vols. I-VI, ed. Charles Hartshorne & Paul Weiss, Vols. VII-VIII, ed. Arthur W. Burks (Cambridge, Mass.: Harvard University Press, 1931-1966). (I follow here, as I shall throughout the chapter, the convention of citing the *Collected Papers* within the text by volume and paragraph number.)

2. This possibility will be considered more completely later in the chapter when I take up a discussion of John Boler's interpretation of Peirce.

3. See, for example, 1.322, 1.323, 5.45ff.

4. John F. Boler, *Charles Peirce and Scholastic Realism* (Seattle: University of Washington Press, 1963).

5. By "Platonic sense" here, I am referring to Scotus' apparent interpretation of the Platonic universal, an interpretation which is certainly open to question.

6. Op. cit., p. 50.

7. Op. cit., p. 64.

8. Ibid., p. 162.

9. Ibid.

10. *Transactions of the C. S. Peirce Society*, Summer 1974, v. X, no. 3, pp. 135ff.

11. Ibid., p. 144.

12. Op. cit., p. 156.

13. Op. cit., p. 144.

14. Ibid., p. 156.

INDEX